On The Edge of Being:

An Afghan Woman's Journey

On The Edge of Being:

An Afghan Woman's Journey

Dr. Sharifa Sharif

Sumach Press

Toronto

On The Edge Of Being: An Afghan Woman's Journey
Dr. Sharifa Sharif

First Published in 2011 by
Sumach Press, an imprint of Three O'Clock Press Inc.
180 Bloor St. West, Suite 801
Toronto, Ontario M5S2V6
www.threeoclockpress.com

All stories in *On The Edge Of Being* are from the author's memory. Names have been changed.

Three O'Clock Press gratefully acknowledges financial support for our publishing activities from the Ontario Arts Council, and the Government of Canada through the Canada Book Fund. We acknowledge the support of the Canada Council for the Arts which last year invested $20.1 million in writing and publishing throughout Canada.

Library and Archives Canada Cataloguing in Publication

Sharif, Sharifa, 1954-
    On the edge of being : an Afghan woman's journey / Sharifa Sharif.

ISBN 978-0-9866388-2-4

1. Sharif, Sharifa, 1954-. 2. Women--Afghanistan--Biography. 3. Afghan Canadian women--Biography. 4. Women--Afghanistan--Social conditions--20th century. I. Title.

DS371.S53A3 2011   305.48'891593092   C2011-905655-0

Cover Design: Gord Robertson
Printed and bound in Canada by Transcontinental

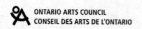

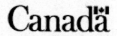

To my late mother, who spoke in silence, struggled in peace, and bonded in separation. And to all Afghan mothers who share her language.

To my father, who gave me the mind to question and treated me no less, no more than himself. And to all fathers who share his path.

Preface

*O*n *the Edge of Being* is a tracing of memories from my own life and the lives of women whose stories have remained vivid in my mind, have touched deep down in my heart and have formed my outlook on life itself. I have known or heard about these women as I have lived in and travelled through different valleys, mountains, villages and cities in Afghanistan, and later as an immigrant in the United States and Canada. Every line in these pages speaks from a real life story.

A lot has happened in Afghanistan since I first began to preserve these stories. The Taliban government was defeated. A democratic constitution has been ratified. The President and members of the Parliament have been elected. The new constitution grants women the right to education, work, the vote and access to political positions. The government has ensured a twenty-five percent female presence in the Parliament by maintaining quotas. International Security Assistance Forces, consisting of forty-eight countries and led by NATO, operate alongside the Afghan national forces throughout the country to ensure security and fight the Taliban and other terrorist elements. Millions of children, including girls, are going to school. Numerous international non-governmental organizations have come to help in the reconstruction of the country. Many of these organizations work for women's advancement. A Ministry of Women's Affairs has been established to ensure the integration of women in the government. An independent commission for human rights has been established, with a separate department for documenting the violation of women's basic human rights and educating them about those rights.

Afghanistan is striving to become a democracy in the midst of internal challenges that make it vulnerable to neighbours' interference: a growing narcotic poppy cultivation supported by influential drug mafia inside the government; a government weakened by widespread corruption; poor economic infrastructure; powerful local warlords manipulating ethnic and regional interests to their advantage; and a seventy percent illiterate population.

Pakistan, the southeastern neighbour, has never been at peace with developments in Afghanistan. Wary of its unresolved border issue on the Durand Line, which has separated forty million *Pashtuns*—the largest ethnic group in Afghanistan—in Pakistan from their tribes in Afghanistan, Pakistan has an apparent interest in manipulating the Afghan government. The Durand Line was the recognized border when, in 1893, King Abdurahman of Afghanistan agreed with the British Empire to leave parts of Afghanistan to the then Indian empire.

During the Afghan *Jihad* and the resistance against the Soviet Union from 1979-89, Pakistan served as the base for international assistance to the *Mujahideen*—holy warriors who fought against the

Soviets in defense of Islam. The Soviet troops formally withdrew from Afghanistan in 1989, but the communist regime of Dr. Najibullah was in power until 1991, when the *Mujahideen* took over the government. It was also Pakistan that created the Taliban—literally, students—as a political force to operate inside Afghanistan. At this time, the Afghan government, NATO forces and the international community are aware of the Taliban sanctuaries, training bases and support in Pakistan.

Iran, another neighbour in the West and an official supporter of the Afghan government's reconstruction and democracy, is engaging itself in a temporary marriage of convenience with the Taliban to support an anti-American insurgency.

Yet, a volatile Afghanistan sandwiched between two radical Muslim nations—a nuclear-armed, unstable Pakistan and an anti-Western Iran, suspected of having nuclear weapons and led by Ahmadi Nezhad—is striving to crawl towards democracy. In the midst of this, the situation for Afghan women has gone through multiple setbacks and political upheavals since I encountered the first woman I tell of in this book.

These first stories I have remembered belong to the earliest chapter of my life in Afghanistan, when political and military stability overshadowed poverty and the inherent oppressive conventions against women and other minorities. There was a slow and disproportionate developmental process, which concentrated on the cities but only indirectly affected the eighty-five percent of the population that lives in rural areas. While there were women in the Parliament, in the cabinet and working as doctors and engineers, oppressive traditions above and beyond the law were silently victimizing a larger number of women in these rural areas and in remote parts of Afghanistan.

It was this majority who then fell victim to the oppression of war, poverty, politics and power. Russian and Afghan soldiers; local warlords; powerful *khans*; poor and desperate fathers, brothers and husbands—they all traumatized and brutalized women in one way or another. The years of war added young widows, poverty-stricken mothers and traumatized sick to the list of those women traditionally oppressed in Afghanistan.

Now, with the eyes and ears of the world open to the story of Afghan women, with democracy voicing its first words and government struggling to function, life has improved to some degree for some women: there are schools, there is work and—more importantly—there is international recognition of Afghan women's rights. The government is now required to enhance participation of women in all sectors and ensure their human rights. There is also a body to watch for the oppressors, hear the cry and voice the concern: the Afghanistan Independent Human Rights Commission.

Nasrin, a young teacher who had to crawl to the prison to see her husband during the Taliban years and was beaten several times for buying food alone in the bazaar, is today attending a teacher's workshop in New York; however, many other young women in her village still do not have the right to go to school. There are still young women murdered for the crime of loving a man, there are still women forced to marry their infant brothers-in-law in order to keep the honour of the household, and there are still many young girls deprived of school, food and care.

Until the gap between the two worlds of women in Afghanistan closes, until education about women's rights reaches the minds and changes the attitudes of ordinary men and women in the most remote valley of the country, until the economic infrastructure is built and until the law can rule outside of the constitution and official publications, for the majority of Afghan women life remains a narrow, invisible path to waste and loss.

My memories are about this majority of people.

Chapter I

The Rainbow of Self

Layers and layers of thick clouds have covered my childhood memories, yet the soft voices, timid faces and quiet hidden footsteps of the women who traversed my childhood are carved deep inside me. I feel them there. I am used to them, although their existence is almost unbearable.

When I look at my face in the mirror, I see a blurred reflection of many colours, looks, shapes and eyes. The story of my life is the same, it echoes many voices, memories and destinies. As I think of my own life and the lives of women around me as I was growing up in Afghanistan, my mind returns vividly to Gardiz, a city of rocks, barren land and dry mountains. From the blurred images of the city, our family life and our time there, certain stories have seized my memory and clung to the story of my life.

Now, in my fifties, as I sit in this room halfway across the world in Toronto, gathering the strength to put my story to paper, it seems that I had started writing my memoir at the age of five.

It was in Gardiz that I would sit on my father's lap and ask him for favours. I still remember the anguish I felt when he told me he would not let me marry until I was twenty years old. I didn't know much about marriage, but it sounded like a long wait for something that was talked about with every girl. Families usually married their daughters in childhood in exchange for money. Some *Pashtun* families gave their young daughters to another family for marriage as compensation or a token of apology for a murder—usually that of a brother or father. This custom is called *Bad* among *Pashtuns* and is a form of public reconciliation, solving lasting conflict and animosity between two tribes or two families. This custom is still practiced among some tribes in rural areas. Of course, I didn't realize then that it was a favour not to be married off; I was very lucky and my father was very fair. Now I know.

When I was five years old, in our living room filled with green and brown cushions, with one door to my mother's bedroom and the other to the corridor, I listened to my father talk about his family and childhood.

It was then, in the filthy room off the kitchen yard, that I first struggled, suffocating, under the heavy belly of our cook. I began to silently watch my own life as it was unfolding before me and its stories as they happened and were told to me. I rehearsed those stories in the solitude of my own bed—a blanket and a mattress spread on the floor next to those of my sisters and brothers, four of us then. My mother gave birth to a child every one and a half years. The newborn and the youngest child stayed in her bedroom while the older children were pushed to the living room.

In those days my main narrator was my father, whose stories

and even jokes sounded like the greatest novels and lessons of life to me. From my mother I heard different stories, usually when my father was away. Those were the times when she was feeling well and in the mood to tell us stories or maybe when she wanted us to see the other side of our kind and broad-minded father. The father that I adored and the husband that she knew were not the same, it seemed. The man who observed life with keen eyes and a big heart and sought justice with a genuine and open mind had different corners and ideas about his marriage and his wife.

To me—the fourth child, second daughter, dark, skinny, fragile and moody—the stories of life began to take shape with characters, voices, patterns, plots and conflicts. Even now, my memory of my mother choking under her heavy burqa in the summer heat is as vivid as my own choking under the heavy body of the cook.

It was there in that house where I was caught by the wild wave of life that turned me into a victim–character and my life into a story. Mine was only one life and there were many victims whose stories I came to hear, but this story of me and the cook was the only one to hide deep in the darkest and most remote edges of my memory. It was in another chapter of my life, here in Toronto, well into my claimed womanhood, that the memory resurfaced and the story was torn from illusion; the fragmented victim–character became part of the whole woman that I am.

The first job that I got in Toronto was as cultural advisor for abused women from minority groups. In one of the training sessions, the facilitator was talking about sexual abuse, incest and child sexual abuse. It occurred to me then that there was no specific word for sexual abuse—or abuse for that matter—in our languages, Pashto and Dari. At least, I hadn't conceptualized my own abuse in any of the languages I spoke, in any term or words; it was a nameless silent burden and a dusty memory, more illusion than reality.

Discovering the term "child sexual abuse" uncovered that illusion for me, and the first story of the abuse and oppression of women in my life became real. This first story of abuse that I remembered was my own. The first abused woman in my life was me, the daughter of my mother; although, strictly speaking, it was my mother, the wife of my father. It was my own buried history, the story of my abuse and oppression, that revealed itself the day I learned the words for it. My abuse had regained its torn space in my life. By becoming part of my memories it had become the missing part of my broken childhood. I had pushed this part of my childhood memory so far back in my mind that my whole childhood had seemed an illusion. Then it was there in front of me, so real, so clear and so vivid that I shared it with the class. After that, it became just another story alongside those of other women, other victims and other abuse that I had carried with me—a story to tell and to share.

It was the summer that I was five when my father, who was working as the deputy governor of Paktia province, was posted in Gardiz. I remember Gardiz with its long summer days. The interminable length and sticky smell of the hours are glued to my memories; those endless afternoons and the air of the kitchen with its agonizing heat and filthy odour still pollute my senses at times.

Inside the house where I lived everything was lonely and long. Even the yard was far too long to cross with a few big jumps. I always wanted to close my eyes, take a deep breath and—Boom!—be on the other side of the yard with my mother. It was a big house with two yards, one inside where my family lived and the other outside where the big kitchen was, where the cook stayed and the security people worked. My brothers and I played in this second yard. It was where we could connect to the outside world, the streets and its people.

The outside yard was frightening. I hated it. I can still smell it. We lived in a compound divided into two sections. The inside house was our private residence, protected from the outside by big walls. In our house we had three big bedrooms, one large living room, a bathroom and a storage area outside in the yard. My mother always stayed inside the house. She never came to the outside yard except when she was leaving the house, which was very rare. My two older brothers, my older sister and I were always playing outside on the street and sometimes in the outer yard.

My sister was smart: she tried to keep my mother's company when she wanted it and played outside when she was busy and wouldn't notice her absence. She knew how to please my mother and play with my brothers, too. I was not smart, I was naive and honest; I was only five years old. I did not please anybody—not my brothers, not my mother, not myself.

My mother often shouted at me for hanging around outside with the boys. My brothers didn't like me because I was upset and cranky most of the time. I did not like myself because I wasn't clean like my sister and my brothers. The filthy stuff was not something I could wash off my body, it was too sticky, it was there on the inside.

It smelled like the dirty kitchen, like our cook, Hasan.

My mother was not allowed to cook because the kitchen was in the outside yard, in a separate unit not attached to our living quarters. My mother was not supposed to see or be seen by any men except immediate family members. Hasan did all the cooking. In fact, he owned the kitchen. It was a very long, dirty, dark room. The ceiling was high and full of smoke. There were stoves made of mud and brick and piles of big black pots in the corner. The whole place smelled of grease, smoke and sweat. It was Hasan's smell.

My afternoons were full of this smell and of anxiety; after a while, I couldn't distinguish the two. Why were there so many afternoons during the summer?

Often, there was nobody around, except for Hasan in the outside yard. My brothers went to school, my father was at work and my mother was with the small children inside the house. I could not resist the temptation to go outside and try to sneak out to the street from the yard. Every time I went outside, there was not one damned person in that long, wide yard to save me from Hasan.

I would look around the yard, my heart pounding. My muscles would tense around my legs as I thought of escaping and jumping over the wall. My body was numb with fear and shame. I was never lucky and never successful: every time I tried to go outside, Hasan caught me. Every time, my prayers failed me and not one soul appeared in the yard to guard me against Hasan. He was so powerful and strong and so lucky—lucky to have me, the one shunned by others. Nobody stood in the way of his afternoon games.

As soon as I entered the outside yard I would look around and every time Hasan would appear right in my way. He would pick me up off the ground and take me to his room. Sometimes, when he caught me, he would just take my hand and I followed. I never said a word. My language would leave me. My mind would sink deep into my soul in guilt and silence. I would find myself in Hasan's room next to the kitchen.

His room was greasy and full of mess; the bed and his blanket smelled, his pillows were sticky, his mattress was hard and thin. He was so heavy and so big that my chest felt crushed under the weight of his body. I felt suffocated and pinned down. It hurt so much. It burned so badly that it would not go away until the next morning. Something piled up inside me that smelled and made me dirty and pained all over.

It never left me, it was always with me—when I played, when I talked to my brothers and sister, when I talked to my mother. I felt guilty when I sat on my father's lap telling him stories. I thought, Why did he not know I was part of such a horrible and dirty game? It did not occur to me then that I had nothing to do with it.

I did not know how and when it started, but I could not stop it. Hasan told me that I couldn't tell anyone about it or he would tell them it was my fault. I believed him. I thought I was the guilty one with bad morals. I thought my mother would believe Hasan and call me a bad girl.

If there had been a world of my own justice, my mother would not have been there. She was cruel. Sometimes, in the middle of dinner, she sent me to go and ask Hasan for a little salt or something. I hated her at those moments. Why didn't she know? Or did she? Couldn't she send someone else, perhaps one of my brothers? I would go, then Hasan would grab me and take me to his bed and lie on top of me. When I brought back the salt my mother always scolded me for delaying so long. I could never eat on those nights. How could I? It hurt so much and smelled so much that I couldn't put another bite into my mouth. I felt filthy and bloated. I felt so angry and miserable that nothing could make me happy.

Hasan's game was so scary. I always prayed that nobody knew about it. I was so afraid that if my father knew, he would kill me. It was horrifying. I was stuck. I knew only one thing that could save me and that was the presence of someone else in the room when Hasan was around. Just one more person. I could not tell my brothers because it was all my fault.

The first time it happened, Hasan told me that if I went with him he would buy me candies and bangles that the gypsies sold. Of course I said yes and after that he became the boss. He had the say. I could not go back. I wished I could, if that were possible. I would have gone back before the first time he lay on top of me.

One day, my father told us that he had been promoted to the governor position in another province. The family rejoiced. I did, too. I couldn't believe my luck. Hasan stayed and we moved away. In the new place—miles and miles away from Hasan—I sometimes had nightmares of him, but he had disappeared from my life. It only hurt when my father said that he had liked Hasan, that he was a good cook and a nice man. He was not, I thought, but could not say. Nobody would listen to me anyway. I was only five years old.

In Gardiz, where Hasan was, there were many other men and women in my life—tall, strong, heavy and rough men. My father was the cleanest, the tallest and the strongest of them all; he was the centre. Hasan was the dirtiest, the cruelest and the ugliest of all. I saw many small, weak, sad, shy and needy women also—my mother the shortest, roundest and weakest. I remember a crowd of street people, all of them poor, vulnerable, cold, hungry and lonely. The streets were full of tall, heavy, loud men and thin, timid, secretive boys. A few old gypsy women sold dairy products or glass and plastic jewellery; still fewer waif-like little girls could be found collecting animal waste to be used as fertilizer.

I never talked to the little girls—I wasn't allowed to. I was the daughter of the deputy governor. The guards would watch me and not let me talk to those "filthy" poor people. I resented the guards for preventing me from talking to the interesting girls, but not protecting me when I really needed it, with Hasan. I felt connected to the street girls, as if our silent smiles spoke a thousand words between us. We had a lot in common: we all liked glass bangles and enjoyed moving our hands to make them sound like metal chains tying the camels in the caravans, we also liked henna on our hands.

I had my problems with henna, too. I would put it on my hands on the eve of *Eid*, the Islamic festival after the month of fasting and pilgrimage to Mecca. Sometimes it hurt and wrinkled my skin. My hands were never as nicely coloured as my sister's. That, along with my hair that stuck out and my dress that never fit as well as hers, made me cry on every first day of *Eid*.

Others blamed me for finding something to cry about on every happy day of festivity. I, of course, blamed my mother. She used to sew our dresses, she always tried to make them loose, why? She never put the right amount of henna on my hands. I had to blame someone or something, and for that, nobody was more vulnerable.

The glass bangles were not easy to get. How far I went to get them is another memory of my childhood in Gardiz.

It was that same summer. I was wandering on the street in front of the house. How I sneaked away from the guards who always stood by the door, I don't remember, but I can still see the gypsy woman passing by, wearing a loose black dress, baggy pants and a long black shawl.

She was carrying a big bag on her head and shouting, "Bangles! Glass, plastic, green and red, blue, any colour you want!"

She noticed me and our eyes met. We spoke: I wanted the bangles. She would give them to me. We bargained: she would give me all the bangles I wanted, the cotton candies, even dresses, and she would colour nice prints of henna on my hands. I just had to go with her to her home and choose from her large collection. I agreed.

She put me on her back and covered me with her big black shawl. I held to her tight with my hands around her neck. She said we didn't have to go far. We hadn't passed the market when someone called my name.

"Yes," I answered. It was one of the guards who was off-duty and had recognized my shoes coming out of the shawl.

My gypsy friend started arguing with the guard, saying that I belonged to her and just had the same name as the deputy governor's daughter. "It is my daughter. She is only a child. What is it with you? Leave me alone," she said.

They started dragging me back and forth with my face still covered under her shawl. I didn't want to let go of her back. I told the guard, "You go! I will come after I get the bangles!"

He got me out of the shawl and took me back home. I hated him for making me break my promise, hurting my pride and stopping me from getting the fancy bangles. I don't remember how my father punished me or even whether he did, all I remember is that he didn't beat me, but rewarded the guard.

After that, my mother injected so much fear into my mind that every time I heard of a girl being kidnapped, a string was pulled in my stomach. She said that the gypsy had tried to take me to sell as a cheap child prostitute in Pakistan or somewhere far away. Even now, when I hear news of child trafficking, that day, that gypsy and that guard are alive in front of my eyes. I was very lucky. Thousands of other girls are not.

In fact, I was lucky in many other ways, too. Most of all, I was lucky to be born to an open-minded father. Had my father been an average Afghan man, I would have been an unwelcome child—a burden or a commodity for sale because of my dark skin and thin body.

My mother told me the story of my birth many times, every time in a different context and for a different reason. I was one of the many births my mother gave at home and with only one inexperienced midwife. I was the third daughter born to my mother; the first daughter had died.

My mother was surprised to see that I was welcomed by my father, he hadn't minded a second living girl. I remember the story well, not only because it is the story of my birth, but also because it resonates with rebellion and challenge: I was welcomed, despite my gender and the colour of my skin. My mother submitted me to the order of the world she lived in, but my father stood up for me. From that day on, it was the story of my win. This pattern continued as I heard more stories from my parents.

Chapter II

A Girl Is Born

My father always complained that my mother was very brief with her words and never told a story completely. With us, too, she was rarely in a storytelling mood, but when she was, the story wasn't brief—she told us every detail. The story of my birth is one of her detailed stories.

One of those days when my mother was in a good mood, she was sewing something in her Zinat manual machine while my sister and I sat beside her. My sister was attending to my baby brother and I was just playing with the yellowish polka dot fabric she was sewing. She wouldn't tell me what she was sewing, but she assured me that it was not clothing for any of my siblings.

That day, she shared with us the story of my birth, her agony about giving birth to another girl and her surprise at my father's reaction. This was my favourite story. I still remember her words and descriptions as well as she told them:

> I was lying on a tiny bed covered with layers of blankets in a small square room that opened through a tall door from a narrow corridor. There was a win-

dow with double doors to the left as you entered the room. Cushions and mattresses filled one side and gave it a cozy look. I had arranged a big pile of blankets and sheets at the facing corner of the entrance door. My metal bed covered with layers of blankets was at the right corner of the room. A small green cradle was hardly visible at the foot of the bed.

The room was filled with the aromatic smoke of burning herbs. The distinct smell of *spand* filled the air—news of a new birth. We believed the herb protects both the mother and child from the evil eye. We also thought that it drove away the devil, who was wildly loose around a postnatal woman, as she would be too weak to resist.

I remember lying in bed with the covers pulled up to my neck and a black scarf tied around my forehead casting the shadow of illness on my face. I had just given birth to my second living daughter, my fourth living child. I was unsure how your father would take the news about a baby girl, not so fair and not so pretty. Dark and tiny.

When mother talked about me like that, my sister would laugh out loud. I resented her for it and asked many more questions about how I looked. It puzzled me why mother had been afraid of what father's reaction would be.

"My father never discriminates between boys and girls. How

come you were nervous about my birth?" I would ask my mother.

I really did not know your father. He had never spoken to me about his feelings, ideas, likes and dislikes. He had only told me a little about the women who liked him and the men who admired his talents. He never asked about my feelings. He was the husband and I was the wife. It was not important what my feelings were. My likes and dislikes hardly mattered. I never asked him, either; I thought it was not my right to indulge in such a conversation with my husband. I just knew that he was tough. I never called him by his first name.

Your father was the son of a famous religious figure and he himself had become a *Mullah*. Then he became a judge, and then deputy governor. At times, he seemed different from other men I had heard about, kind and considerate. At other times, he was just a typical husband: demanding, strict and suspicious about me. He was good to the poor, but this was probably because he had been poor once. He was devoted to justice and fairness among people, but his relations with me were not so just and fair. He did not consider my feelings at all. He didn't seem to care that I had a family far away that I missed terribly, that I wanted to go out occasionally and meet another soul, perhaps some women to chat with, that I wanted to buy nice things for myself and my children.

I was a young woman married at the age of sixteen and was fifteen years younger than your father. Who was I to know about justice and injustice—to judge a judge? I was only the wife. I was not even literate. It couldn't be less than a hundred times a day your father reminded me of this and pointed out that I didn't know anything.

I didn't like it when mother made my father sound like a bad husband. I didn't want to know that face of him; he was a kind and good father, so he must have been a good husband, too. He was in many ways, maybe, but not all. Every time my mother spoke about my father in his role as husband, I changed the subject. I wanted to hear the part about Father's uniqueness, not his commonality with other men and husbands.

"So, tell me again how Father came to know about my birth?" I asked my mother.

I remember, when I gave birth, my thoughts were swept between sleep and exhaustion. The midwife who helped me felt cursed at having to give the bad news to my husband. In her experience, when she gave the husband news of a baby girl, she wouldn't get a tip for her services. I knew this much: your father wouldn't blame me for having a daughter. But, how he would feel inside and how he would take the news was not so predictable.

The midwife cleaned the baby and prepared a drink for me. Then she burned the herbs that would spread the news of womanly business around the house and send the men away. The midwife wouldn't even let my little boys come to my room for a couple of days after I gave birth; birthing is women's work and women's business and it is considered shameful.

The midwife waited anxiously until your father came home from work. She stood in the doorway. Your father appeared at the door and the midwife lowered her head.

"*Salam,*" she said softly.

Your father must have sniffed bad news. He probably thought I had died in delivery like his first wife or maybe he was afraid there was something wrong with the baby. He could not wait to know, but didn't want to show his anxiety—a weakness for a man in his position. Smiling calmly, he asked if everything was okay.

The midwife shied away. "Yes, but..." she murmured.

"But what?" my husband interrupted.

"It is a girl, sir," the midwife whispered with guilt.

Oh, your father's reaction shocked the midwife!

"Stupid woman! You think a girl is not a human being? You think I would discriminate against my own flesh and blood? Get lost!" His voice shook the midwife. Many other reactions would have been more expected, but this... The startled midwife stepped aside to let my husband enter.

I took a deep breath and smiled with relief. Once again, my husband seemed different. Later, my family got the word of my dark baby girl and they started worrying for me. But at home, everything seemed okay. Your father did not mind a girl at all. He said a boy or a girl was the same for him.

This was my mother's story about how I—the fourth child, the dark and depressed one—came into this world. From that day on, I grew up a lucky girl who belonged to an unusually open-minded father, but my mother remained a vulnerable wife at the mercy of her husband. The tide of my mother's life rose and fell with the changes in her husband's mood; she never got the strength to acknowledge herself or to rise above the waves.

I felt like a wild branch growing from the trunk of an ancient tree. My mother was the tree, spreading her blood and flesh into many branches. She gave birth to eight more babies after me. My father became the supportive, considerate, open-minded man in my life. He never treated us—his daughters—differently, he never denied us the rights my brothers had and he never mistrusted us.

I grew up loving him as a father, but deeply resenting him as my mother's husband. The husband and the father were two separate people. My mother understood our delusion about the fair and just father that we had, and the strict and tough husband that she had. When she was in a happy mood to tell us stories or even unhappy with my father, she told us about her first years of marriage—her hard life, hard work and my father's strict rules. Both my parents told us stories of their first years. My father usually told his stories after dinner to all of us, which made my mother uneasy. My mother told her stories in the absence of my father, during the day, to whichever child she was with.

There were fifteen years difference between their ages; my mother was sixteen when she married my father. He always told us about the first time he met my mother after the wedding—they hadn't met, but my mother had seen him through the door crack when he came to ask my grandmother for my mother's hand.

He said that when he saw my mother for the first time after the wedding, he was a bit taken aback by his bride's young age. Most of the ceremony was carried on separately for men and women and the bride wore a thick, colourful shawl covering her face during most of the ceremony, even though there were only women.

"Oh, you are so young and small!" was my father's first reaction and first words to my mother, he told us.

"I am not," was my mother's response, he said.

This was the way my parents' married life and communication had started: my father's questioning and my mother's self-defence.

It was probably from that day on that my mother strived to prove herself—first to her husband and, through him, to the family and to society.

My mother told us many stories of her struggle to be a good wife. These stories had always been alive in my memories, but when I went back to Afghanistan while the *Mujahideen* and their rules were dominant outside Kabul, I had to wear a burqa in the summer heat and a particular memory of my mother's suffocation under the shawl hit home.

Chapter III

Marriage on Trial

During the early 1960s, an extraordinary event occurred: the government declared that women could appear in public without wearing the veil. Then, it became a game for kids to chase the women who still wore *chadaries*. Since my father was the governor of the province, he was the first man to carry out the new laws. My mother had worn a *chadari* until that time, but then she became the first woman in the province to appear unveiled, in public with my father.

Women were supposed to wear dark sunglasses, a scarf on the head and long gowns. I was too young to worry about *chadari* and I had never worn it anyway. For my mother, however, it was a big break from her earlier days when my father was a judge and she was completely covered.

Thus, my mother became unveiled, but she could hardly believe she was out of the cage of *chadari*. To her, my father was always the man who determined her boundaries; suddenly, the government had stripped the women of their *chadaries*. It was, overall, a thing to be glad about, but the sense of exposure that came without warning was shocking. I think it was hard for my mother to feel the good part of this new kind of independence when it meant she was unexpectedly visible to all men, to all of society. I imagine she felt it brought a kind of responsibility for which she was not prepared.

When I asked her about it years later, she said she was not nervous about revealing her face to the public, but she was very nervous about how to hold herself so my father would not find fault with her. She said, "I wanted to look around and see as much as I could without a veil. But I was wary of my eyes and my looks. I thought your father was watching every movement and turn of my eyes."

It was our custom: women could never be sure if the good they perceived was actually good or not. "Good" was only what a man had dictated and, as such, seemed to have very little value in and of itself. It wasn't just about new laws governing clothing—a woman's physical being, her very life, was treated in a similar manner.

However, as I grew older, my father became less strict about my mother's appearance and life became easier for her. She then cared less about the big scarf she wore around the house, wearing it around her neck or resting it next to her on the floor or a chair. She stopped covering her face or running to the back room when a male servant came in to bring something, she would just grab a scarf or pull a piece of cloth over her head.

I can still picture my mother with a grey nylon scarf around her neck, one hand on a piece of fabric, another turning the sewing machine handle, telling the story of her first ever trip outside her village, and my father's strict adherence to the veil and covering.

I left the village for the first time after I married your father. It was summer and thirty-two degrees when we were traveling from our village to Jalalabad, where your father had gotten a job. I was sinking in sweat and heat under my nylon *chadari*. The truck was jammed with passengers, one on top of the other. The women were tightly covered, head to toe, in *chadaries* and closely guided by their husbands or brothers throughout the journey.

Our journey felt very long to me. In reality, it was only about two hundred and fifty kilometres from my village. The roads were not paved then and the trucks were going very slowly. My mother had advised me to be an obedient wife and respect my husband.

I liked the stories of my mother's married life, or perhaps, I just liked my mother telling stories to me. But every time I heard of my father's harshness towards her, I felt angry. A strange sense of resentment, rejection and denial overwhelmed me, but I didn't know who to resent, what to reject and what to deny.

My mother was an easy target so I resented her. I felt angry at her, and even hated her, when she told stories of how she had put up with the oppression. She and her stories sparked a feeling of hatred deep in me. It created doubts about my father. I couldn't afford that. I trusted my father; my image of him had become the wall of protection against abuse, my distrust and hatred of the outside world. Destroying this wall would destroy the safe world I had built inside.

All of my grandparents had died before I was born. My father would tell us about his parents all the time. I could picture my paternal grandparents and my father's childhood clearly in my mind, but I had heard very little about my mother's childhood and parents. She would answer my questions briefly when I asked of her life before marriage, but didn't talk much about her parents or her own childhood unless she was in one of her rare storytelling moods. That required free time and free thoughts, which she didn't have much of.

When I heard my mother's story of her first trip, it was only then that I realized my grandmother was alive when my mother left her village. How could she be separated from her mother so far away? I felt sorry for her.

"Was your mother alive then?" I asked her.

She seemed annoyed by my question or by my ignorance about her family.

Of course she was. My mother was a very young widow with five children. She had my older sister married off and then me, too, while I was still very young, to lessen her financial and social burden. A young widow with two grown daughters and two young sons was vulnerable to gossip and hardship. Because my husband-to-be was handsome and well-recognized as a government official, my mother didn't hesitate to accept his proposal of marriage for me.

"What about you? Did you like my father?" I asked.

My mother was very reserved about her feelings; she wouldn't describe them directly, but she would hint at them. She had never directly said she had liked my father when they first met, but this time she somehow admitted it:

> I'd seen him through the cracks of the door when he came to our house to propose. A few days after, we were married and he wanted us to leave for Jalalabad, where he would work. It was my first trip outside my village—my first introduction to the outside world.
>
> What I saw was not much. I could see only a few feet ahead of my steps through the holes of my burqa. I felt burdened with heat, shame and anxiety. I was anxious not to embarrass my husband, not to do something wrong, commit a sin, not be a shameful woman in front of all the strange men on the truck. When you have just become a wife—especially the wife of a strict, highly respected judge—you become vulnerable. Any single gesture I made, anything that seemed unwomanly, might be held against me.
>
> I didn't want to do anything wrong. I was careful to keep my *chadari* wrapped tightly around me and to close even the smallest hole that might let in a breeze. My husband draped a woolen blanket over my *chadari*, an appropriate extra covering for the wife of a judge. My skin crawled beneath my dress,

my *chadari* and the woolen blanket. I couldn't deflect the heat. My husband's rough coughs warned me of my disobedience. Only later, during a beating, would I learn that I was not to move beneath my clothing and wraps. Moving attracts attention, moving draws the attention of men.

What could create greater shame and guilt than asking for attention? Why could I not be quiet and still so men could forget my existence in the sweltering crowd of the truck and continue their afternoon daydreams uninterrupted? I felt hot and suffocated.

After we arrived at our new home, after the beating, I understood my husband's frustration. In public, I was not to move beneath my clothing for fear this would be misinterpreted as a gesture soliciting attention. These gestures are sinful for a woman and dishonourable for my husband. I couldn't convince him that I had only been trying to adjust the *chadari* so that I might catch a little bit of a breeze. He was angry and I felt guilty for making him so. Needless to say, I didn't go outside much anyway, but when I did, I wore the *chadari* properly. I was completely veiled and covered and never let any of its edges become loose or untied.

The first years of my marriage were stressful. I moulded myself to my husband's wishes and rules. It was a one-way relationship: he was at the top giving commands and I was at the bottom obeying them. Our marriage consisted of his words and wishes only. I was anxiety-ridden in my attempts to obey my husband. I had to read his mind, it was a necessity of life. As a woman and a wife, I was to be completely hidden from every man, except my own brothers. I strictly abided by this law.

My husband had many visitors and they were received in the only room we had. During these visits, I was confined to the kitchen at all times, so he would come to fetch the tea or dinner for the visitors; if even the smallest sign of me were visible, he would raise hell. When he came home with visitors, I would spend hours wondering what I was supposed to do: Prepare dinner? Make tea? How much of my time would that actually take?

Once we had a visit with an old man from our village who was also a relative of the family. He stayed with us for several days. During the day while my husband was at work, the guest and I were alone in the house—he in the only room we had and I in the kitchen. I would prepare a tray of food for him and leave it behind the door. Then I would knock to signal that it was ready. He would come for the tray after I had walked away from the door.

One day, I took him some warm water for him to wash himself and softly murmured through the door that it was waiting for him. After the visitor left, my husband beat me and asked why I had allowed my voice to be heard by a strange man. His question puzzles me to this day. How did he expect me to attend to his guest in total silence and invisibility?

Then, and even now, Mother's anecdote and Father's anger at her puzzled me.

It was only few years ago, decades after my mother's time, that I witnessed a similar dilemma about women's visibility. I was at my cousin's house in Kabul. She is married to my other cousin. One uncle's son had married another uncle's daughter, both from my mother's side. For Afghans, like for all Muslims, cousin marriage is acceptable. In fact, it is very common and considered safe; it is understood that knowing family background and lifestyle is the safest and easiest way of creating harmony among couples.

My cousin had brought his friends home—unexpected guests for his wife. He took his friends into the guest unit outside the house, but it was just next to the kitchen so that when she left the kitchen window open, she could hear them. It was a warm summer evening. My cousin and her daughter disappeared into the kitchen and started cooking for the surprise guests. I was sitting in the living room with the younger kids.

When the dinner was ready and her husband and young sons took the food to the guest unit, my cousin got the chance to come to where her little kids and I were sitting. Her daughter brought food for us and my cousin sat to relax after a couple of hours of non-stop cooking.

She started laughing with a bitter sarcasm. "I can't believe my husband," she said.

"What has he done this time?" I asked.

"It is so hot in the kitchen. He is angry that I opened the window because his friends could hear me and could tell I was in the kitchen. Isn't it funny? Who do they think cooks for them, genies?"

We both laughed, but my cousin's struggle to keep her husband happy resonated with my mother's stories of her first days of marriage in Jalalabad. It amazed me how some beliefs about women can live through generations.

The only difference between my cousin and my mother was the asking of a question: my cousin was asking her husband not to hide her very existence, even in the kitchen, but my mother never questioned my father. She accepted a life on trial, only questioning her own skill and potential for being a good wife. This was echoed in her stories about the first years of her marriage.

I can still hear her soft voice.

I felt like marriage was an ongoing examination of my survival skills. To have a husband and to keep him pleased was a test that I seemed destined to fail.

Then there were children. The expectation was that I would have many of them—a son first, of course—

and raise them the correct way. My first daughter died while my husband was at work in Jalalabad and I was in the village. I had no connection to the city or to a hospital.

My daughter died of diarrhea, despite my pleas to my brother-in-law to bring medicine from the city. He wouldn't listen; he told me to give her herbs. When she died, I had nightmares about my husband blaming me for the death of our child.

After my daughter's death, I could not conceive. I desperately sought treatment from anybody and everybody with ideas about fertility: herbs, shrines and black magic were all suggested to me. The pressure and anxiety of infertility lasted four years.

During this time, many people offered their daughters and sisters to your father to be his wife. Luckily, he didn't accept anybody. Finally, God gave me a son. Your eldest brother.

"So did having a child relieve you of the stress of Father being unsatisfied and marrying another woman?" I would ask Mother when she told me the story of her first child.

She replied, "Not really. I knew he wasn't the kind of person who would marry another woman, but the stress of meeting his expectations and of being a good wife still remained. It did not decrease as my children were born and added to my mothering responsibilities. No matter what went on in the outside world, inside the house we remained a traditional husband and wife who lived on the edges of the husband's mood. I had a child every two years, God keep them. Two dead, plus many miscarriages. Now, as I am older and the children are growing, your father has softened a bit."

We, the children, grew—some noisy and naughty, some quiet and calm, some violent and some depressed. I, personally, was not treated badly by my father, though it seemed like my mother was.

It did not matter whether I was beaten or not, there were thousands of other ways that I got hurt. I heard stories of other women who were hurt or insulted by the system, by their husbands and fathers, by laws and beliefs. Each of these stories hurt me. I heard them from my father or from my father's friends. I learned, however slowly, that simply being female justified the unfairness of it all. And the women around me accepted it.

Chapter IV

Punishing Laughter

I was a disillusioned child, bearing the burden of shame and guilt. As I grew older, I saw abuse and harassment wrapped tight as a scarf around women's necks. Life was full of abuse, full of unfairness and one-sided relationships. Only pain penetrated the soul, all else skimmed along the surface. The huge men who forced their bodies on top of tiny girls; the moody husbands who pulled their wives behind them, dragging them to the doorsteps of their adultery; and the angry mothers who took their frustration out on their children and pinched them and pulled their hair, beat them and kept distant from them—all were signs of abuse. They had all suffered from abuse and transferred it to their offspring, the younger generations.

As a child, I did not know whose side I should take at home, my mother's or my father's. My mother was never close to me and never drew me close to her. I resented that. My father was fair and kind to me, but hard to my mother. Sometimes, when my father was cruel to her in front of me, I just got more confused and didn't know who to blame or to whom I should turn for help. But I knew for sure that something was wrong and somebody was to blame.

It was almost impossible to think my father could be wrong, so I became numb and cold when he was cruel and I tried to find fault with my mother. This way, life could be easier. I chose to believe that my mother's illiteracy was to blame, not my father's temper. I believed that even if he is cruel and unkind, the one who knows everything and brings food to the family can punish the ones who don't know the outside world.

I wish it were that easy. It was never that smooth, it was complicated. If I didn't take sides, it hurt me inside and made me angry. If I did take sides, that hurt, too, and made me wary of myself. If I blamed my mother, I felt ruined, shattered. If I blamed my father, the world seemed out of order, everything fell apart. Either way, I was never able to trust myself.

One night, during my father's next assignment as a governor—far away from Gardiz and Hasan, when a new sun was shining over our heads and life seemed brighter—my mother attended a wedding party, taking my sister and me along. The women were celebrating inside the big house and the men were outside in the guesthouse and yard. Everything was segregated: the dinner, the music, the decorations. However, when the bride and groom sat for *nikah*, the groom came to the women's side and the female guests got to see him. Inevitably, a few other men glued themselves to the groom in order to be admitted to the women's side as well.

Many women among the guests were veiled and had come to the wedding on the condition that the men and women would be entirely segregated. My mother was one of them. My father was governor of the province at the time, and she was the first lady. I remember her face as young and happy. She tried to connect with the newly married couple by showing her emotions, her joy, publicly. She was trying to participate, to say something, to offer suggestions to the bride about details of the ceremony—where to put the bowl of holy drink, where to put the mirror in which the bride and groom would see each other's faces for the first time. I could tell she was enjoying herself. My mother was not permitted to go to such occasions often. When she was, it became a major event for her and for us.

That night, for the first time, I felt my mother was showing signs of being a whole person: she talked and laughed, expressed her happiness and congratulated the bride and groom. The ceremony lasted well past midnight. By the time we got home, my father and brothers were waiting for us. We entered the house and sat in front of my father and brothers. My father began the inquisition.

"Why are you so late?" he demanded.

My mother countered with whatever excuses she could think of to explain why it had taken so long to get home. To rescue my mother from the onslaught of questions, I tried to change the subject and started talking about the bride and groom without realizing I would trip a wire in my father's mind.

"So you sat there and watched that young man and the other men who accompanied him? You looked at them?" he demanded.

I felt a stream of sweat run down my body. My father threw

pillows at my mother, blaming and scolding her for her insolence and stupidity, her overt lack of respect, her purposeful socialization with men. This was the first time I saw my father physically attacking my mother, and my mother being attacked with no defiance.

That night, and nights like it, were the carving knife that whittled the images into my soul.

That my mother had come home after my father was the first warning bell that sounded; this was quite abnormal and smelled of wrongdoing or transgression on my mother's part; some untied connection, something that had come undone.

I always felt my mother's anxiety in such situations. When she felt her husband had noticed something suspicious, she immediately assumed the guilt. She would search frantically and blindly for a corner or a hole in which to hide. I remember vividly my mother's helpless efforts to defend herself, and with that I recall my anger about her lack of self-respect. As a child, I don't think I could understand why she might have felt survival was more important. I didn't understand that in the woman's world in which I lived, these things were mutually exclusive.

Our new house in Sheberghan was free of the scary yard and Hasan. My memories of him and his bed slowly faded away as life settled down with new people and new places. I was introduced to friendship and girls came out to share my days. Life acquired wider dimensions as more people came into view; trust gradually pushed away the bitter taste of fear in my relationships with people. I saw faces and smelled smells that were different from Hasan. These faces mainly belonged to the young girls who became my intimate friends.

I was six years old and my sister was ten. We met some girls who were our neighbours and the daughters of other government officials like my father. They were my sister's girlfriends, but I was the younger sister and was attached to her and the places she visited. My older sister and I started school at the same time. We both enrolled in the first grade since there had been no girls' schools in the previous province where we'd lived. Soon my sister transferred to a higher grade.

My sister made new friends in her class. At home, we developed an intimate circle of close friends. There were twelve of us and a few were also sisters. The older sisters created the games and rules. We played husbands and wives. We made couples with each other. The older ones—with more authority—became husbands, and the younger ones—the weaker ones—became wives.

I played the wife with another friend. We played the whole game as far as we could go. It was easy to be a wife because the husband had to make all the decisions, but it was the wives' duty to always be pleasant and that was hard. We slept together; it felt warm, intimate and safe. We kissed each other on the face. We hugged each other and touched each other's bodies. It felt good. Nobody knew we were playing husbands and wives, but every time we played it, we felt guilty. I was afraid of my parents. In fact, I was afraid of any enjoyment I had: playing outside, shopping, laughing loudly on the streets or even chasing the mad man.

Chasing the mad man was another naughty game in our group. My mother always told us not to chase him because it was both a sin and a shame. But whenever we were by ourselves without any sign of our brothers, we looked for him, found him and chased him. The madman was short and small and usually wore a piece of cloth that flowed loosely around his frame. People thought he was crazy because he always kept to himself. He did not have a home or a family of his own. Every time we chased him, we shouted at him, "Mad Man! Mad Man!"

He lured us to hidden places. When he was totally hidden from other grownups, he exposed himself to us. His huge penis would stick out from under his gown and we would shout and run. I remember the sight of it was terrifying, as if he were about to kill us or do something really dangerous. We little ones would try to run away, but my sister and the other older girls would push us toward him and laugh. I don't remember why we chased the madman. It wasn't much fun, but we persisted in doing so anyway.

Chapter V
New Laws, Old Beliefs

As my father was transferred to different provinces, we travelled with him and saw many different places. We also heard many stories that confirmed my beliefs about women's oppression. How these stories might have been analyzed with the cultural and societal logic of that time does not seem relevant to me today; what matters was the reality then. The stories were of young girls, young women and elderly women trapped in various injustices.

It was not as if being released from one's duty to wear the *chadari* created a true kind of freedom. It was bizarre. Ultimately, a woman just had to assume another kind of veil; there was no protection anywhere. For some reason, my father always seemed surprised by this.

The number of my siblings had grown to seven by the time my father was transferred to Urozgan, a most remote and underdeveloped tribal province, which to this day has not modernized. Urozgan was not industrially developed, but it was naturally striking. Its mountains stood rigid and high, its rivers flowed full, its people lived with love and pride. It breaks my heart to know that, industrially, Urozgan is still the poorest province in Afghanistan. Even worse, the landscape and people are now crushed in conflicting wars. That once green, clear, simple valley that had been the setting of my childhood memories and captured my young imagination has now become a desert of killing and destruction.

When my father became the governor of Urozgan, there were no schools for girls in that province. He opened one, but since it was new it only had first grade, and my sister and I were in grades two and three. No school was not an option for my father so he asked us to join the boys' school. This was unheard of—segregation in schools at that time was as rigid as schooling itself—but, we had to study, so we went. After us, some other government officials followed and send their daughters to the boys' school. I joined grade two with Mehri, the daughter of the security chief. Going to school with boys felt natural to me, then.

Mehri and I sat in the very front row and shared a bench. During the recess we tried to avoid the boys, but we were kids and easily forgot our boundaries, so we mixed and played together. This changed when we grew older and went to higher grades. My sister and the daughter of another official were already in higher grades; they were teenagers, and more vulnerable and sensitive to their gender.

Everything was normal and smooth in school, but at home my mother often reminded us of the boys in our classes and how critical it was for us to stay reserved and distant. We did stick to our front row and tried not to look back, but our classmates were very nice boys, they used to pick apricots for us and assured us of their protection if we needed it.

One day, Mehri and I were expecting our classmate, Wahab, to bring us some apricots, but he was late to school that morning. We were standing in the line up in the yard, listening to the principal who was talking about discipline and how he will punish latecomers and other wrong-doers. When he asked for the victims —students to be punished—to come forward, I was very upset to see Wahab stepping up with his hands in his pockets. The principal was cruel, I thought. He used to make fun of students in front of the entire school and then beat them with sticks—on the palms of their hands if it was a lesser sin and on the soles of their feet if it was major. The principal would ask the students to lie down on the ground with their legs raised. Someone would tie their feet together, then the principal would start beating them until the sticks from the branches broke.

That day the principal asked Wahab to lie down, Mehri and I were scared. What if he told the principal about the apricots? What about them? Why we were so scared, I don't know now, but at the time my heart was pounding and my palms were sweating from fear and shame.

The principal made some sarcastic comments about how important and intelligent Wahab was and then started beating him on his feet. With every stroke, the stick made a sweeping noise that ended in a click when it touched his soles. I don't remember how many blows hit him, but it seemed countless and the sweeping noise continued for hours.

Wahab was twisting his butt with every strike and crying, "I won't be late again! Damn me!"

In the midst of his twists and cries a roar of laughter broke. The principal started making fun of him again: "Now we see what an important job you had! So this is what has made you late!"

The laughter grew louder. Mehri poked me and pinched my arm. I peeked through the row of students from the higher grades who were standing in front of us; apricots were rolling away out of Wahab's pockets. Nobody dared to pick any up, but everybody was looking at them.

My heart almost stopped. This was it, I thought. Now Wahab would say he brought them for Mehri and me. He would say we made him steal the apricots. But he didn't say anything. The beating finally stopped. Wahab's feet were untied, he grabbed his vest and slippers, stood up stiffly, threw his shawl onto his shoulder and started limping toward the class. His eyes avoided Mehri and me. We felt guilty and embarrassed. We were distant for a few days. But then he started bringing those delicious sour apricots again and we were friends.

Every time I hear about the Taliban burning a girls' school in Urozgan, I think of my school days there. Some memories are sweet, some bold and some bitter. There were many questions raised then; many answered, more still unanswered.

Our teachers were all men. Most graduated from the ninth grade of that same school, some from the twelfth grade at schools in Kabul. One of our teachers was Dad Mohammad Khan. He was very highly qualified, having a twelfth grade diploma from Kabul. He was tall and wore a brown suit to school. I think he was our geography teacher. In one of his classes, when we were left to study on our own, I got very bored and wrote a note to Mehri, who was sitting next to me. I didn't think much about the note, but I wanted to do something and engage Mehri. Nothing came to my mind. I wrote, "Teacher Dad Mohammad is very tall."

While I was slipping the note to Mehri, he saw me. He came and snatched the note from my clenched hand. After scolding me, and making fun of me in front of the class for writing notes and not studying, he took the note to the principal. It was a big deal, a big crime that I had committed. Soon my sister knew about it. Everybody talked about it.

The next morning, the principal lectured about it in front of the entire school, without naming me. He said we should not make inappropriate comments about our teachers. I didn't understand then, and don't even now, what the big deal was about the note, but my sister thought that it had implied a compliment and was therefore inappropriate.

There were other disturbing memories of days at that school—days that I wet myself in the class, hoping nobody would notice. There was one traditional bathroom, which I don't remember well. We girls would usually go to the bathroom together during recess. Our classes were from eight in the morning to one in the afternoon, with one recess around ten. During the classes, I never dared to go to the bathroom. It would be very obvious where I was going and that was so embarrassing and so bold that I never asked. I would hold it tight, tight until it hurt.

When it hurt too much or my bladder could no longer hold it, I would let it go. First a little, then a little more and then all. Disaster. I would remain still for the rest of the time and pray that my loose and baggy pants would hide it. When I got up, I hoped Mehri would not see the wet spot on the bench. Maybe she didn't; she never mentioned anything. Those days were the hardest to go home. I was sure my mother would notice even if she didn't say a word. She never did.

Didn't she know? Or, was she embarrassed for me? Or, maybe she didn't like it but didn't voice her dislike. That was my mother. Her relatives often praised her for her ability to withstand hardship and pain without saying a word. It was true; she had a massive tolerance for pain. Even when she gave birth to her children, she never raised her voice or said, Ouch!

My mother gave birth to two more sons in Urozgan, both at home, with an untrained midwife. We kids didn't know or talk much about my mother's pregnancy. She, herself, treated it as a shameful secret. My older sister would tell me that my mother was pregnant. On the day or night that she was to deliver we would suspect something.

"It is a boy!" or "It is a girl!" was the news we would hear.

On that day or night, the midwife would sleep with my mum.

We kids would sleep together in another room. We either heard a baby cry or saw my mother's head covered with a black scarf the next morning. I only remember that one of my brothers was born at noon in Urozgan. The midwife was there. My father told us before he went to the office that morning that my mother was giving birth to a new brother or sister. I was playing with my friend, pretending to be carefree, but I was worried and scared for my mother.

We were not allowed to go to her room, but I made excuses to pass by the door and have a glance inside. It was around noon that my eyes caught my mother standing in front of her steel bed. She was holding on to the frame tightly and gasping in pain. The midwife saw me, and quickly closed the door and told me to go away. Then I heard some noise and panic, and my brother running to call my father. My mother had lost a lot of blood and she had fainted. Soon, Father came with the doctor. He was happy; he gave us some money for the good news that my mother had recovered and the fifth son was born.

Chapter VI

Zulaikha

Tribal laws were dominant in Urozgan, but government laws were also making their way into family life and relations. There were two prisons in Khas Urozgan, the capital city, one for men and one for women. Women would usually be punished by their male guardians before they came to court, but the government did occasionally interfere. Most of the time, women wound up in prison for crimes of adultery or for escaping abusive partners three times their age. In a way, the prison was a kind of protection and shelter for these women, no matter how misplaced justice seemed.

The province was poor. In the entire capital city there were two cars: one for the governor and one for the security officer. Radio was rare, a luxury reserved for government officials and very rich landlords. There was no electricity. The government authorities had appointed my father to the province because he was a *Pashtun* and had good insight into both religious and traditional issues. I lived there from the age of six until I was twelve.

We lived in a big house, with a huge yard and a servant quarter where the kitchen was. The cook was usually a soldier who was somehow excused from military duties and was passing time doing domestic work. This kind of soldier worked in the houses of the governor or other high-ranking government officials.

There were some female domestic labourers who served as maids for the governor or other officials. These women were usually prisoners doing time. They were given food, shelter and clothing from the households where they worked. The prisons in the city were poor and underequipped, with minimal shelter and necessities. One women's prison served the entire province. More than a dozen women slept in one small room and their food consisted of bread and scant vegetables. Meat was rare and there was seldom enough for everyone.

Male inmates worked construction for long hours during the day under the tight security of the guards. Female inmates were the most vulnerable group, without relatives, money or work. They had no choice but to tolerate anything and everything, as often they had been sent here from distant villages. As a way to assist the lesser offenders among these women, they were taken in as maids in the homes of the government officials.

Zulaikha was one of those women. She was working for one of the security commanders, my friend Mehri's father. Their house was right next door to ours. Mehri usually shared her family's secret stories with me and sometimes complained about her strict father. She said her father never spoke to them, the children, and only to her mother when he felt like it. The rest of the time he was in his room by himself and did not want to be disturbed. Mehri had three brothers. Two were younger than she, but one was the oldest child and very spoiled. I spent a lot of time playing with Mehri in her house.

Zulaikha was always busy with baby care, washing clothes by hand in the yard or cleaning. She was very pleasant and full of laughter and joy. Unlike Zulaikha, Mehri's mother was mean and unhappy. I remember that almost every day that I was at Mehri's house, I heard her mother scolding Zulaikha and yelling at her. Zulaikha was playful and talkative and wanted to talk to Mehri and me and laugh with us, but as soon as Mehri's mother heard Zulaikha laughing, she would start screaming at her about why she was wasting her time with laughter and talk and avoiding doing chores.

Zulaikha told us many times about her first day in the prison.

It was one early morning two years ago when I was brought to the prison. I was twenty-one and from a remote village. The women in the prison circled me as the guard pushed me through the big door to the rectangular yard. I had a small bag with me that I hid under my shawl. The women tried to make me feel at home: one brought tea, one sweets and dried fruits, whatever they had that their visitors had brought them. I sat quietly, aloof in the centre of attention, and was bombarded by questions from the other women. Some were friendly, some annoying, some hostile and some kind.

Mehri and I liked Zulaikha's stories, but we wanted to know more. We wanted to know why she was in prison. What was her crime? To us, only criminals—murderers, robbers and dangerous thieves—were imprisoned. Zulaikha didn't seem capable of doing any of those crimes. She was too kind, too pleasant, too sensible and sentimental to kill, steal or rob. But we were embarrassed to ask her. I sometimes wished I didn't know she had been imprisoned; knowing made her a criminal within my value system. It didn't feel right. Mehri and I tried to picture Zulaikha committing crimes that would put her in jail. None would go with her personality.

One summer afternoon, when Mehri's mother was taking a nap, her brothers were gone to the market and Zulaikha was patching her clothes, Mehri and I felt it was the right time to ask her. It felt like popping a surprise question. I finally got myself together and asked her about her crime—or sin, as we considered it. She smiled and paused for a moment, and kind of shook her head and said we wouldn't want to know. But we insisted and she told us the story.

> I got married three years ago. My husband is very old. He can't do anything. I took care of him for three years, even though I hate him, because I needed food. I needed clothes. You'd think he could get me those? Forget it. I finally ran away from the old, wild pig after three years of putting up with his bad moods and beatings. He couldn't make me sleep with him, he was too old, and even if he did, I wouldn't have wanted it with him. I needed love and sex.

Hearing her talk about sex and sleeping together with her husband made me blush and feel embarrassed inside. No adult would talk to us about sex or sleeping with men so directly. Even my sister wouldn't talk about it in front of me. These words were taboos. Only shameless and loose girls would talk about such things. We were too decent to have such talks.

But the way Zulaikha was telling us the story engaged me with suspense and interest. We kind of giggled, twisted our legs and got closer to her.

My neighbour's son was coming to help us and run some outdoor errands for us. He was very young and handsome. Nice, too. Well, we liked each other and started having an affair. We were doing it right inside my house when my husband was asleep. Once he fell asleep, he never woke up—but that night he did. He caught us. I am paying for it now. What the hell! At least I had a few good nights. If only they didn't do this to me. Well. That night, I served my husband his dinner and waited till he fell asleep. He used to fall asleep so fast that at the beginning I thought he was faking it, but he was a heavy sleeper. It was rare that he awoke after he fell asleep, but that night he did.

That night, I still remember. A summer night. It was hot. My husband was sleeping on the roof, where we all used to sleep in the summer. My boyfriend and I had planned to meet after dinner was done and my husband had retired for the night. I saw my husband falling asleep and waited till I heard him snoring. I then waved with my shawl to my boyfriend who was waiting for me outside our house, behind the wall. He came and we rushed to have our secret romance in the only room. I don't know what got to my husband that he woke up that night. Not only that, he walked down the roof and, well, probably heard us, and walked right into the room and stood above us. It was such clear moonlight that we could not hide behind the night. We were there rolling on top of each other right in front of his eyes.

Zulaikha threw her head back and burst into laughter. When she pulled her scarf to cover her hair, I noticed that a piece of her right ear was cut. I pinched Mehri and looked at Zulaikha's ears. She had noticed it, too. We each silently expected the other to ask the question. Mehri was wiser than me; she didn't ask Zulaikha about her ear, but asked if she had been punished by her husband. Zulaikha looked surprised.

He would have killed me, if he was able to, but he was very old, sick and weak. He groaned above us in rage. He didn't really know what to do; he was shaking and kind of spinning around himself, as if he was looking for something to hit us with. But before he came to his senses, my boyfriend disappeared out the back door. He left me to deal with my husband who was scolding and throwing anything he could at me. He railed at me till dawn then went to the mosque as usual. But that morning he returned with two relatives: his brother-in-law and a cousin.

I knew his brother-in-law. He was a very cruel

man. His wife, my sister-in-law, always complained of his bad temper. He used to beat her so badly that sometimes she couldn't move for days. He wouldn't let her go anywhere, anyway. She was the only living sibling of my husband, but came to our house only once a year, for *Eid*. I always felt scared when I saw him.

They all walked to our room in silence while I was in the kitchen preparing breakfast. I knew I would be punished somehow, by somebody. I was so busy worrying and baking bread for breakfast that I never saw them coming. Someone grabbed me from behind and covered my eyes. From the size of the hands and the roughness of the grab, I could tell it was my husband's brother-in-law. Everything happened very fast. I felt a sharp pain on my nose and tasted blood running into my mouth. As I was struggling to release myself, his hands covered my face and tilted my head. Then I felt a burning inside my ear. I don't know how long I was passed out, but I came to my senses right where I had dropped. Blood was everywhere—on my face, on my clothes, in the kitchen.

I was hurt and miserable, but happy that that was it for my punishment. But then my husband told the police, anyway. Two days later, they came to our

house and took me handcuffed to court. Then they
sent me to prison.

I hadn't noticed the cut on Zulaikha's nose until that day, or if I
had, it looked like a brown scar to me. Now, after hearing her story,
Zulaikha looked like and became a different person to me—she
had a piece of her nose and ear cut, but she was not a criminal. It
was a sin she had committed, but it wasn't a crime. In our court
of justice, Mehri and I acquitted Zulaikha. She was guilty only
of sin, which connected us all beneath our skin. My sister would
sometimes scold me for talking to a prisoner so much, but to me she
was a nice, warm, loving woman. I thought of Zulaikha a lot then
and remember her even now.

She had endured prison life for five years. It went on and on. She
rarely went to bed with a full stomach. The women were always
given such small rations, never sufficient for an adult. But such was
life until something changed for Zulaikha and she was brought to
the commander's house. That was another question we asked Zulaikha, by what fortune had she come to Mehri's house as a maid.

She remembered that day for us, too.

It was early one fall morning. Some women were
sitting outside in the yard, sipping tea and making
routine gossip about the prison guards and officers,
some were inside cleaning the floor. I was sitting
against the door mending old clothes. We all became
alert when the officer opened the big metal gate and
walked in with the guard. He didn't come to us un-

less there was news: a new prisoner, a release order, bad news for an inmate or the like. Sensing news, we became all ears, anxious to see how it would change our routine. The officer said a few typical greetings and, in his authoritative tone, broke the news, saying the Commander's wife needed help around the house. She wanted to keep one of us as her maid.

He said, "You'll share their food and tea and water and will sleep in their house. In return, you must help the lady of the house with the chores and take care of the children."

When he finished his news, he looked around the yard to examine us: the younger ones were covering their smiles with the corners of their scarves, the older ones were looking straight at the officer's eyes. There was no sign of dissent from the women, nor had the officer left room for it.

He looked at me. I was still holding clothes on my lap. "What about you, Zulaikha? Are you fast enough and smart enough to work in the Commander's house?"

I didn't know what to say or even what it would mean for me. I looked around for answers from my cellmates. They all shouted, "Go, go, you can do it! Yes, yes, officer, she is very good. She is good at cleaning, also. Yes, Zulaikha, go and bring us the stories."

One of the young women, who was usually aloof and didn't get along well with the rest of us, took a step toward the officer. "Can I go, Mr. Officer?" she asked.

The officer looked her up and down. "Mmmmmm. I don't think so," he said. "You really have to be very clean and neat. You will stay here."

The young woman murmured something and stepped back to her place. The officer turned his back to leave. Just as he was walking out the door, he said he would come back in half an hour to get me. I was to get ready. And here I am.

This was Zulaikha's story of coming to Mehri's house.

Then, Mehri told me how it was on the first day Zulaikha came. She said for her it was a big day to hear that a prisoner woman was coming to be a maid. Mehri remembered that on the first day, as Zulaikha sat inside the living room door with her big scarf wrapped around her, Mehri's mother, the lady of the house, stood in front of her.

She looked Zulaikha up and down several times and asked her a few demeaning questions: "What are you good at? Have you done any cleaning? Do you know how to care for babies?"

Zulaikha whispered responses, but the lady didn't care much

for her answers and started to chat with the officer. Zulaikha was ignored.

It seemed like it didn't take very long before Zulaikha was burdened with dozens of chores and services. Every time I was in Mehri's house, I saw her running back and forth from one chore to the next, from one person to another. The little kids asked for attention and carrying, and the grownups asked for everything: from having their ironing done to bringing them a glass of tea and cleaning up their messes.

Zulaikha could manage those types of chores without much difficulty, but with the adult males of the house—the Commander himself and his two sons, sixteen and eighteen years old—the chores were very different and tricky. They wanted more than domestic service. They wanted sex at their convenience.

Zulaikha became more occupied with the chores and the work. Mehri and I thought she was either avoiding us or that Mehri's mother told her not to talk to us. Mehri said that Zulaikha had become distant. Whenever Mehri and I were together and sought her conversation, she made herself busy with something. We wondered what the reason could be.

One day, when Mehri herself seemed unusually preoccupied and aloof, I probed and probed and made her talk. She told me she had seen something she couldn't believe. I insisted and she shared it with me.

She said she saw Zulaikha coming out of her father's bedroom while her mother guarded the door so the kids wouldn't go in. It was confusing and hard to believe. Was Zulaikha sleeping with Mehri's father with her mother's permission? We couldn't comprehend such a thing. We tried to swallow this incident and blame it on some odd coincidence or something. But we both became more alert, especially Mehri because she lived there. Another day the same incident took place, and Mehri got angry and confused and shared it with me. This happened again and again and again.

Mehri was now angry at her own family. She said her older brother was doing the same thing, except her mother didn't guard for him. He would just yell at her and demand a task: ironing his shirt, bringing tea or something. Then Zulaikha would go inside and he would lock the door behind her. Later, Zulaikha would come out blushing, embarrassed and nervous.

Mehri and I planned to witness the next episode of Zulaikha's affair with her father together. One afternoon, when Mehri thought her father would take the afternoon off, we planned to stick around. Mehri stayed inside. I went to see her. Her father was in his bedroom. Her mother nervously tried to make Mehri and me go out and do something in the yard, but we made excuses and stayed in. Mehri's mother walked around grumbling for no reason, not even making sense, just nagging at Mehri about how she always played with her girlfriends and didn't study. Zulaikha came with a tray of green tea, dry fruit and a few cookies. I said Hi to her. She murmured Hi back, without looking at me, and walked towards Mehri's mother, who, while standing by her husband's bedroom door, gestured toward it with her hand and snapped at Zulaikha to go in. When Zulaikha went in, Mehri's mother yelled at us to go out and play and leave her alone. We did.

Mehri and I were angry, confused and ashamed. Mehri told me how she could see her mother's resentment and hatred towards Zulaikha. She said Zulaikha never looked her mother in the eye after she came out of the bedroom. The two women always avoided each other's eyes at those times.

We thought there was an unspoken bond between them, then; they were both victims. Mehri's mother never admitted her own shame to Zulaikha. Instead, she would simply ask her to "Take some tea in for Sir, the Commander."

We were sure Zulaikha had felt the rage in her mistress's voice and she quietly did what she was told. While Zulaikha delivered the tea and performed the rest of the task, Mehri's mother walked away in haste and pretended to be busy. Mehri said it was usually the day after Zulaikha's invitation to her husband's bedroom that her mother would take all her anger and hurt out on Zulaikha and give her hell. This abuse continued for a year.

Before the next winter approached, Mehri came to see me with a piece of news: Zulaikha had been taken back to prison. She said her mother had called the officer and told him that she wasn't satisfied with Zulaikha's work anymore. She had told the officer that she would appreciate it if he would pick an older woman next time, since the young women were rather carefree.

So, Zulaikha returned to prison after a year of service at the Commander's house. During her remaining days there, Zulaikha looked pale and heavy. She seemed quiet and worried. After she was gone, Mehri told me that she overheard her mother talking to her father about Zulaikha's pregnancy, but her mother wouldn't tell whose child she was carrying. We wondered if they knew. I wondered whether Zulaikha knew.

Zulaikha had told us her life stories. She had told us stories of such heartbreak that we had almost cried for her, but she also spoke with so much fun and laughter that we enjoyed it thoroughly. Mehri and I then grew angry with men, at husbands who could be so cruel and so lustful. We were angry with her mother, who was so submissive. Mehri's mother was an obedient wife: powerless and selfless toward her husband. But she took out her frustration on Zulaikha. She herself was imprisoned in the marriage, having put her dignity, her desire and her inner womanly pride aside for her husband. Had she not done so, she would have been pushed and pulled and pinched by the Commander. For her, pleasing her husband was not a matter of five years incarceration—it was a life sentence.

We were also mad at Zulaikha for agreeing to it, but then we realized she didn't have a choice. She probably couldn't think about wanting or not wanting such attention, she just thought about how to handle it while not offending the lady of the house. Zulaikha was trapped and afraid. If she rejected the men, she was in trouble the next day and punished with curses and insults. The Commander could influence decisions about her life. If she didn't reject the men, then the lady and the girls of the house bombarded her with taunts, verbal assaults and physical abuse.

What happened to Zulaikha and her baby, God only knows.

Once the women were behind the tall, gloomy walls of the prison, they were totally hidden from the public.

I often wondered which prison was worse: a woman's own home or the prison itself where food and shelter never sufficed, and where abuse and insecurity abounded. Perhaps the worse prisons were the homes of the officials, with enough food and shelter, but more chores and sexual, emotional and physical abuse. I wondered whether the women themselves could ever sort it out.

Chapter VII

Gem of the Valley

U rozgan was the valley of hidden beauty and buried hopes. Hopes grew in buds and withered before they bloomed. The young heard about the outside world but were trapped in their remote valley away from the cities. Women heard from the radio or from relatives and friends who knew about living conditions in the developed world, that people in the cities and mainly in the West had better lives, but they were still used as doormats.

I bonded with nature in those years in the valley. Early mornings, when I accompanied my father on his hunting trips, the high rugged mountain and the river flowing from its belly spoke to me of serenity and the abundance of time. Now that I relate to life and living through nature, I see that the rocky slope of the mountain and that wild flow of the Urozgan river were its first calls for me. I didn't mind that spot for short early morning trips, but whined when my father took us there for picnics. My idea of a picnic spot then was a green park and gardens of flowers.

On those quiet and serene mornings, my young mind tied together the loose ends of stories that I heard from my father, my friends and the friends of my mother. My father went hunting for geese and ducks at dawn. Usually my brother went with him, but I had to compete with him and wake up early in the morning so I could go. Some nights I tried very hard, begging him to wake me up so I could go with them. I went only a few times. The first time I was there I spotted a man, a peasant in the village on the other side of the river. My brother had told me about a guy crossing the river from the village and bringing breakfast to them every morning when they were there. I felt bad when I saw him holding a tray above his head in one hand and keeping up his rolled-up, baggy pants with the other as he struggled against the waves of water. He finally managed and came towards us.

When my father noticed him, he murmured, "Not again! This poor stupid man is taking so much trouble."

The man greeted my father, kneeled down and put the tray in front of us, bashfully saying, "I hope the milk is not cold. My wife just milked the cow and baked the bread."

"God bless you! You shouldn't do that," my father answered with an annoyed voice. There were three glasses. I looked proudly at my brother. The man had noticed my presence and counted me, too; it wasn't my brother alone accompanying my father. The bread and milk smelled good and fresh. My father asked us to hurry and finish eating so the man could return to his house.

When we finished, my father thanked the man again but he didn't sound appreciative, we thought. He asked him not to bring us food again. My brother and I felt bad, we thought Father was cruel and unappreciative. After the man took his tray and went to cross the river to his house, we asked my father why he had been so cold to him. He told us that he didn't want the man to feel obliged to treat the governor every time he saw him. He told us that the man would be happier if he didn't bring the food, but he thought it was his duty to take food to whoever showed up around his village as a guest, especially a governor. We didn't agree.

I went hunting with my father a few more times. Every time we went, I felt the dawn when the sun had not yet stretched its arms around the earth, and the lilac valleys were especially fresh and clean underneath the thick cover of trees. The sounds of nature were light but deep: lowing of cows and calves from the barn, calls of the rooster and soft songs of early morning birds. Amidst those sounds, I imagined the painful cries of women: women beaten, tortured, abused and imprisoned, women in labour and dying of it. There, I was connected to nature and to people.

One day, a girl named Gem was brought to our house in Uroz-gan. Later, when I heard the story of her life, I imagined hearing her mother's cry in childbirth during one of those early dawns. Gem was Taher's daughter. Later, we heard from him that Gem's mother had died giving birth to her at their farmhouse, far away from the city. Tehar had named her Gem because she was very beautiful and seemed unique and bright to him, so bright and beautiful that Taher didn't think his house deserved to be her home. He wanted Gem to be above and away from their poverty and isolation. He worried how he would ever be able to secure this bright girl's future. How could he make opportunities accessible to her? He also thought about his own well-being. Poverty had no end. Hardship never jumped its tracks. He thought of Gem as a doorway to safety and a bright future for both of them. So he decided to make her a gift, a priceless and precious gift to a well-off household with good parents. She was not given a gift; rather, she was given *as* a gift.

Taher thought everybody would understand the value of this priceless gift, especially the governor, my father, whom he liked so much. Taher later told us how he respected my father and connected with him when he heard him speaking their language and taking the side of the poor in every situation. He also told us about his agonizing thoughts regarding Gem's future. But one early morning he left his village with a decision. He reached the city just before the grand meeting of the governor began. Representatives of the people were to speak. Taher announced his decision about Gem there, in public.

I heard about Taher and Gem from my father after he came home from the grand meeting that day. My father had arrived a little later than usual. He usually told us about his day at work after drinking his tea and listening to the news, but that day he called to my mother as soon as he got home, telling her that he was trapped. We were surprised. My father never spoke of any trouble at work, he was always on top of everything, he was a success, people liked him, his superiors respected and trusted him, he was confident and proud of his honesty.

"What happened?" my mother asked.

My father looked at us—my sister, brother, my mother and me—and said, "It is very serious. Listen carefully. It is a matter of honour, life and death."

We couldn't wait to hear what had happened. My father sat in his chair, asked for his tea and for me to close the door, and said, "At the meeting today, after I spoke about my plans for the province and the representatives spoke about their needs and problems, a man named Taher from the valley village asked to speak. I had seen him once before when I was visiting his village. At first, he praised and appreciated me for my integrity and leadership. He then publicly announced that he was giving three personal gifts to me: a fast, healthy horse, a piece of land and his beautiful little daughter."

"What? His girl?" my mother almost shouted.

"Yes. His girl!" said my father. Shaking his head, he continued, "Yes. He said he was giving me his girl. It was up to me whether to marry her to one of my sons or just keep her as my own foster daughter. The public applauded and I was speechless. What could I say? There is no way to reject the gift. I couldn't afford that. It would be extremely insensitive to do that. In this province? With these people? They are rigid *Pashtuns* who kill for their honour and dignity."

My father, himself a *Pashtun*, would always tell us how, for them, land signifies social rank. A girl signifies their personal, familial and social honour. Nothing can be more insulting and dishonouring than rejecting the gift of a girl.

My father said he thought for a moment of the best possible response. There was nothing he could do but accept the girl. So he thanked Taher for his generosity and trust. He didn't accept the land and the horse, but accepted the girl with honour. He promised Taher to raise his daughter like one of his own.

How could he reject this gift? How could anyone reject a young girl? She was much more than a gift to reject and yet much less than a horse or land to own. She wasn't adding to our family's livelihood, like the horse or the land would. She was a different kind of asset, more valuable in some ways, but more burdensome in others.

Thus, Gem was brought to our house and became part of the family. She was seven years old then, a tiny little girl with big dark eyes, thick lips and a tall, slim, refined figure. She just added yet another member to our household.

I had four sisters and five brothers, and Gem did not have a clear position among us. She wasn't really adopted, but wasn't a stranger either. There was an unspoken expectation that she would be married to one of my brothers, but to have a beautiful young girl in the home of a stranger was simply not acceptable—not to Taher and his family, not to his villagers and not even to our family. Gem was socially undefined. Her father had not argued explicitly for her to be married to one of my brothers, but he had implied it. It was the nature of such a gift; even the public knew this.

Now Gem was physically in our house and my father and mother had to decide to which son Gem should be engaged. My oldest brother was studying in the capital. He was too good and too intelligent to be entrapped in this mess concocted by my parents. The second son, Hakim, was also away studying, though he was still too young to prove himself. The other sons were much younger than Hakim, who was twelve. My father decided to betroth Gem to Hakim. He wrote to Hakim to explain the awkward agreement.

He read his letter to my mother:

Dear Son,

I am stuck with a very sensitive and complicated situation. A father in the village has given me his daughter as a gift to one of my sons. You are my rational son. You will be the future husband of this innocent girl. She is very young now. I will do my best to give her a proper education and to make her a good match for you. It's a very sensitive issue; any rejection in this respect will have serious consequences for all of us.

And so, Hakim and Gem became unofficially engaged. Everyone waited anxiously and critically to see what would happen with her.

Two years later, my father was transferred to the province of Ghazni and Gem was packed up with the rest of us to move to our new home. Since the new province had a high school for boys and girls, my brothers also came to stay with us. Gem became a more noticeable addition. Everybody asked about her relation to us. We couldn't say sister, and didn't want to say sister-in-law. Our social life extended to larger circles, occasions and events. Each time there was a guest, Gem's story was told and received with sympathy, pity and suspicion. Gem was growing up listening to the story of her own life as her adoptive family told it.

Hakim knew Gem was his fiancée, but he never connected her to his future. For him, it was a story that took place in the past during his father's official service in the previous province; it was a story that belonged more to his father than it did to him. Hakim became resentful of the responsibility his father had imposed upon him. He realized that his name and future had become permanently attached to Gem, he had no choice. He did not resent those who made the story and made him part of it, but he did begin to resent, and even hate, Gem.

As we grew older, the girls began to realize where we stood in the social order while the boys began to understand their position as young men in the family. In every little boy's head, there are pictures of a future life and a future mate. Hakim had his own fantasies: his mate would be a new person, somebody he wasn't already living with, somebody who was not a sort-of-sister-sort-of-fiancée, somebody he had not yet met.

Gem's position was really very uncommon and she could not be easily removed. At times we thought of her as just another face in our crowd, but just as often my mother openly showed her disgust at having to raise someone other than her own too-numerous children. To my father, though, Gem was the living embodiment of his honour, the honour of her father and the rest of the men in her family, and even the entire village. She was like an organ that cannot be removed from the body; she could not be returned to her family without consequent revenge and death. Shame, of course, was inevitable. Therefore, nobody dared to think of sending her back, but it was our unspoken wish and possibly hers as well.

Our household was growing with relatives coming to live with us. Gem was no longer the only "extra." When my uncle left a wife and three young children behind, my father felt obligated to support all four, as an Afghan is socially expected to support his brother's widow. A sister-in-law—the brother's wife—is a man's honour just as much as his own wife. My uncle's widow and her three children made Gem's presence as an outsider more obvious. There were too many people in the house who were not part of the immediate family.

To make matters worse, Gem was diagnosed with tuberculosis. Everyone in the house then resented her. It wasn't her fault, but it seemed like it was. Perhaps we thought it had something to do with her village background. We travelled very often, too, and she was a problem every time. She was carsick and we put her down for it: we weren't sick in the car, she wasn't like the rest of us. For my brother who was engaged to her, it engendered a fierce resentment. He was a teenager in love with cars and this was just a big embarrassment.

Years passed. Gem went to school with us, she slept in the same room with us, her future was not discussed. Hakim was growing up, too. Gem was totally excluded from the picture he imagined of his future. She was not part of his social life.

For Gem, the hardest part was that, as part of the family, it was her duty to attend to guests. She often had to serve the girls who came to visit Hakim. Then she was a family member, but nobody recognized her engagement to Hakim. She remained excluded until she could no longer ignore thinking about the future and a partner. She developed an outward bitterness just as she was growing into a woman. Hakim didn't notice her beauty. He was looking for love and beauty in anybody but Gem.

One day, Gem finally revolted. She asked my mother to end the drama of her engagement. "Acknowledge me or send me back," she demanded.

Hakim said no to the marriage. He resisted the threat of her father's possible desire for revenge. My uncles heard about the problem and came to make him change his mind and prevent this dishonour and shame on our family. They argued that people would taunt us for the rest of our lives for sending away our honour. To them, this was worse than divorce. My mother pleaded, stating what she had invested in Gem.

We were divided. Some of us supported Hakim and some supported Gem. My father flatly dismissed Hakim's rejection and once again ordered him to marry her. Humiliated, Gem said she wanted to leave. The family was shocked. My father was furious that my brother rejected her; his conscience could never be clear of her.

One evening, my father told us something which, even to this day, I cannot fathom. He said he had agreed with Hakim to ask Gem's father to come and take her back to their village in Urozgan.

My mother explained that Hakim had a long discussion with

my father and had convinced him that Gem was no good. We were shocked. Gem was beautiful, smart and had been raised in our household. What could possibly be wrong with her? What could be so serious that it made our father accept this dishonour?

Later I heard from my sister that Hakim had told my father that Gem was not a virgin. To us, it seemed a flimsy and probably phony excuse. To my father, even the idea of such a thing was valid enough to make her acceptance more shameful than her rejection. Now my father could kill her or her father for bringing such shame to our family, but he didn't do that. Instead he asked Gem if it was true. She admitted that she was raped by one of the male servants in the house.

This was the story as I heard it from my sister. The story did not come from our father, Gem, Hakim or my mother. If Gem had ever truly been a branch on our family tree, she was about to be chopped off.

Gem sent a letter to her father. Ashamed, disgusted and disillusioned, her father came to fetch her. He also had bad news for Gem: her brother had died. Gem went back to her village. Nothing happened. Nobody killed anybody. Gem and her drama were soon forgotten. Hakim married one of his girlfriends, a modern, educated young woman. My father felt content and accomplished. Gem's father felt like a failure, rejected and refused.

Hakim's wife was my classmate, but I thought about Gem. Part of me doubted the story of her stolen virginity. I still don't know the truth.

The last thing we heard about Gem was that she had gone blind. Everybody felt guilty about it, even Hakim... for a moment. I thought her womanhood would be empty if she hadn't any vision. I reflect on the irony now. Vision? What is vision? It is to see clearly, to imagine the future. The blindness of our lives stunned me each time I thought about Gem. More and more, I felt sightless because of it. And then the worry: how can one know if one is blind, if one can never see? It was as if Gem's blindness closed my own eyes and turned my gaze inward. I began to see the featureless terrain of my childhood against the background of my culture, my sex and my country.

Years later, after I had gone to university, the words of Simone de Beauvoir stayed with me. She wrote: "One is not born, but rather becomes, a woman." At the time I read them, the words seemed alive with meaning. But when I hold the memory of Gem up to these words, their meaning leaks out and away.

Chapter VIII
Womanhood and Guilt

I remember the first seasons of my adult life as the scattered and gloomy scenes of a lost dream. My childhood went by with a sweeping wind of guilt and hurt inside, my body bent under a load of secrets. From the moment I could touch the sand or feel the water, I became aware of being a girl, of not being free like a boy to play and be myself. There were strings attached to everything I did and experienced. The sand I played in, the dirt and dust that covered my hands and face, the sticky mud on my feet—these all became symbols of a sullied and soiled life, of what it meant to be a girl.

Being female was like being wrapped in guilt, with its heavy fabric never dropping from my back, though occasionally it would slip a little. I would always bend over to collect it, never knowing exactly what I had done wrong. I could hear my mother's angry curses and feel my father's disappointed gaze. The only thing I knew for sure was that if I had some fun, it was something I wasn't allowed to have. No matter what I did, I felt that maybe my simply existing was the thing that was really wrong.

I felt insecure and inadequate. I was the fourth child and got blamed for everything. I was told I wasn't beautiful compared to my older sister, who was fairer. I guess that was something else I knew for sure: I wasn't beautiful.

I vividly remember holidays and festivals where every child in our household was happy with their new clothes and shoes—everybody but me. My new things never made me look as good as my sister. She was pretty, I was not. Her new things added to her fashion sense, mine did not. I wasn't happy even though there seemed to be a kind of happiness around me. It seemed shallow. I was not satisfied with the world. There was no order, or maybe the order of things was simply unfair; it all favoured men and boys.

My sister never seemed to mind. I thought that maybe if she had taken my side we might have been able to change the order of things, but she never gave me the chance to say anything about it to her. She said I was too strict and stubborn. She asked me why we should bother ourselves with remaking something that had already been made for us.

For my older sister, life was easy. She did not feel pain when my mother scolded us for playing outside like boys or for not cleaning up after our brothers. Somehow, my sister understood my mother's language much better than I did. I would be offended and resentful of my brothers when my mother asked us to do things for them, but my sister would just laugh out of boredom with our brothers. I used to think this was a betrayal, that she was hiding something from me. When we played together, she seemed just like me, she even had the same desires I had, but still I could not fathom how she could be laughing and playing with our brothers while my mother was telling us we had to be at their service and obey them. I was hurt when I was told to clean up after my brothers even though they never had to do anything for me or for my mother. I would cry when I was punished for having fun and my brothers were not. My sister would tell me that it was okay.

Nobody, to this day, has ever given me a good reason for why it was okay for me to serve my brothers and not the other way around. All they said, and still say now, boils down to one thing: you are a woman, they are men.

It wasn't easy to pass through the stages of puberty. It was expected that when girls reached puberty, they should become shy, modest and secretive about their bodies. We were only taught that puberty was about becoming sexual, all the other physical and mental development was not important. For girls, puberty signified reproduction and our identity was forever tied to this. For boys, however, puberty indicated manhood, a superb social identity that suggested the activating nature of masculinity. Families would speak proudly of the growth of their son's beard and moustache, but the daughter's menstruation was a silent shame. Even their breasts were embarrassing.

I still walk with a hunch because of the bend I imposed on my spine to hide my breasts. I had seen other girls of our family cover their breasts with a scarf, but I didn't wear one—my parents did not ask us to and I didn't like to wear one, anyway. To me it was another imposition on women that I didn't agree with. My walk probably wasn't hiding my breasts, but at least I was undermining them. It was body language that conveyed modesty.

Having breasts was not nearly as embarrassing as menstruation. I had only heard my mother allude to menstruation as a period of impurity—in fact, she never talked openly about it at all. It was so dirty and so shameful that it never came up as a normal issue, it was just one more thing wrong with women. Birth was also full of shame: breasts, blood, love, sex, pain. Guilt. But menstruation was definitely the worst thing on the list.

We were told that women had these problems because we were subordinate to men. If we were not truly subordinate, then God would have given some of these shameful problems to men. Men live in a pure world of activity and piety; they solve the problems of the world while the women are there for them, in their beds, to relieve their lust. Women bear the consequence of this. Women cannot be whole and complete, especially in their sexuality. Some women referred to menstruation as a "pray less" time, since Muslim women are not allowed to pray and fast during menstruation. Since my mother never mentioned menstruation as a normal phase of our growth and development, she did not give us the courage to talk about it with her.

My nightmares about sexuality and womanhood grew from wild stories I'd heard as a child—stories about monsters, creatures, snakes and lizards coming to a woman's grave to punish her. I thought that a woman's life was meant to be full of pain, profanity, shame and guilt. From the moment she came into the world, a girl brought disgrace and guilt to her mother. As soon as her genital organ was shaped like a vagina, she was a potential embarrassment to her parents. If just one man saw her naked body, her mother would be blamed and cursed. A girl was ready for marriage as soon as she reached menstruation. My uncle's wife told me that she had her first period in her husband's house after she got married. Though this is somewhat unusual, my aunt was probably not the only woman who found herself in such a situation.

We were told that during menstruation, God cannot reach you. You do not mention it to your elders. Men are never to hear a word about it. During the holy month of Ramadan, if you are menstruating, you cannot fast, but don't eat in front of men folk because then they can tell. While every other Muslim is pure and close to God during Ramadan, a woman's fast is broken the minute she menstruates. She is defiled. All aspects of a woman's sexuality—even her fertility—are to be hidden.

The wedding night is supposed to be the peak of a woman's sexuality and identity, when her virginity signifies her value and she becomes accepted as a wife. Yet what I heard about the wedding night was full of pain and anxiety about the loss of virginity. Nobody talked about the excitement of lovemaking. They only instructed: it is so painful, but you do not cry. It is your pride. Your mother-in-law will take your bloody underpants the next day and show them to her relatives as proof of your virginity.

I learned all of this from other people—girlfriends, aunts and sisters—but never from my mother; she did not talk to us about these very private matters. I heard many things about women's misfortunes. I heard that giving birth was just one more unbearable experience for women. Stories of horrifying experiences during the wedding night and childbirth replaced my fantasies about marriage and motherhood. My older sister and her friends did not seem to mind these stories so much, but for me they were hair-raising. How I envied my brothers! Of course I wanted to be married and have children, but I didn't want to have the pain and hurt and shame. This fear stayed with me.

One day, when I was thirteen and in the sixth grade, I noticed red spots on my underwear. I could not believe God was doing this to me. Menstruation! I felt as though the whole earth and sky had fallen on my shoulders. How was I going to hide my shame from my parents and siblings? Every few minutes I checked and there was more blood. It never stopped. I ran to the toilet to cover it with dirt and soil, as we had traditional toilets and used sod for cleaning ourselves.

I wasn't aware of sanitary napkins and neither were my friends and their families. I don't think they'd reached my country at that time. We used cloth rags for our periods and then we washed and reused them. It was hell trying to do this work and keep it hidden. I can still feel the fear of almost being discovered. I prayed to God deeply from my heart. At that time my father was the dearest and the most important person in my life, but still I proposed a deal with God: I asked him to let my father die in ten years but to not reveal my terrible secret. Fortunately, God didn't hear me.

My mother finally found out I was menstruating, but she did not discuss it with me directly except to suggest that I be more careful and not let my things be noticeable. She also implied that because I had started my period earlier than my sister I was not as decent. It was a sign of my being outgoing and too open, perhaps too sexual—bad qualities in a girl. Thus, I entered womanhood a little faster than the other girls in my family. The guilt followed me into my adult life, into my romances and my fantasies—everywhere.

As my sister and I grew older and our schooling became more advanced, we needed to go to the girls' high school in Kabul. My father was transferred to a different province, Jawzjan, where he had worked once before and where I had gone to school for the first time. It was different this time. I was in grade nine and my sister in grade ten. There was a girls' school in Jawzjan, but it only went up to grade seven, so my father sent my sister and me with my brother to Kabul. There we had a house and my father arranged for a housekeeper who could cook and clean for us. I was the youngest of the three.

Kabul in the 1970s was considered a modern city in the region. Some tourists would have found it full of contrasts, with the most traditional ways right next to the most modern, but to us it was a normal city. It had what we wanted: schools, university, cinemas, shops, restaurants, parks, radio and so on. We didn't have television, but didn't miss it much.

My sister and I were in high school together, where we prepared for university. Once we entered university, we would be studying with men. In my mind, I was still connected to my mother and her way of doing things. But I was also hearing fragments of stories from other women and their desire for love and life. Gradually I made friends with women who had relationships with men. When they shared their feelings with me, so many more things became real. And not very much later, I felt love and passion within myself.

I was romantic. I read fiction and poetry and thought about deep love. My favourite love stories were tragic, one-sided and highly idealistic. I perceived love in remote abstract tragedies. In retrospect, I was drawn to abusive situations. Now I am told it was a result of the abuse I experienced in my childhood. Now I can see how the sexual abuse I suffered—the guilt—had left such a scar in my mind that it obscured real love and relationships. A real mutual loving relationship with a man had become incomprehensible to me. There were only untold and unrequited crushes with unreachable young men, married men, men in love with my friends. None real, none accessible.

Chapter IX

Pieces of Love

I was still in high school when my father was transferred to the province of Kunar, another underdeveloped and conservative *Pashtun*-dominated province. It was actually where my father's ancestors had come from; they had migrated from Kunar to Shamali, the northern region of Kabul. Kunar was another untouched place of natural gems. High rocky mountains in some regions and abundant green pine trees in others made it unique and a popular tourist attraction.

Every winter during school holidays, we went to Kunar to stay with my parents. My younger siblings, who were in elementary school, lived there with them. The holidays were long the winter after I graduated from grade twelve. We had taken the university entrance exam and were waiting for the results. After weeks of agony, I learned from my brother, who was in Kabul, that I had passed and been accepted in the faculty of Literature, which was my first choice. There were student demonstrations that year about the university regulations concerning student assemblies and required grades for the entry exam, so classes were suspended. We graduated in December and waited until September to start university. That was when I stayed in Kunar, heard stories, met people and saw life in an extremely poor province.

In Kunar, there was a girls' elementary school that went up to grade six. In Afghanistan, elementary school went from grade one to grade eight and high school started at grade nine and went to grade twelve. At the girls' school in Kunar, the grades went up with the students: as they successfully finished one grade, the next grade opened for them to attend. When these students passed grade six, the school opened grade seven. After I left, I heard that the girls went up to grade eight and stopped there. The government claimed that it did not have enough in the budget to change the elementary school into high school with grades nine to twelve. Later on, it did become a high school. There were only two female teachers, which was surprising to me, coming from Kabul where there were numerous girls' high schools and qualified female teachers in search of a job. My father suggested that instead of waiting in boredom and agony for the university to start, I could teach at the girls' school.

My first day in Kunar Girls' School was full of surprises and excitement. The office was a long room with an uneven floor. A short man sitting at the only desk in the room greeted me. He was wearing a white turban, brown striped jacket and dark khaki pants, and had a long beard. He looked mischievous, but was a smiling, pleasant man. There was one old, white-bearded man wearing the local long dress and baggy pants, and another young, thin, dark man wearing black pants and a grey jacket. They all wore the same clothes every day of the three months that I was there.

There were also two ladies who were happy to see me, especially the younger lady, Laila, who was the rich *khan's* daughter and later became a good friend of mine. The other was an older lady who was almost illiterate but was teaching the girls about the Quran and Islam. I could hear girls giggling behind the door. Every now and then one would come, peek in and run off, followed by the laughter of the others. They were curious to see their new teacher, the daughter of their governor.

I started teaching grade six literature. Soon I made friends with many of the students. Most were my age or even older because they had only enrolled in school when they were teenagers; before that, there was no girls' school in the area. Hawa was one of these girls. She was beautiful and smart. Unlike most of the others, she talked about the injustice in women's lives. She told me stories of her friends who had been forced to marry or given in exchange for settling a dispute. She also talked about poverty and hardship. Most of all, she read poems, sang songs and talked about love.

Hawa was the star of her class and school. She rarely skipped school, but when she did, everybody noticed her absence. There was a pressing reason every time she had to skip. She was living with her elderly father, young brother and two younger sisters. Her mother had died of tuberculosis.

One day, with the spring and midterm exams approaching, Hawa didn't come to school. Then another day, and another. The fourth day she showed up late, looking sad and aloof. She said she was sick, but then at the end of class she followed me to the car where the driver was waiting to take me home. She knocked on the window and shook a piece of paper at me. I rolled down the window. She said she had a top-secret letter for me and pushed a crumpled piece of paper into my hands.

I read the letter on the way home. After greeting me at length and begging me to keep her secret, she wrote:

Dear Teacher,

I am sharing this with you because you seem to care about women's lives and the injustice. I am sure you know how much passion I have for learning and school, but the reason I have been absent lately is that I am in big trouble. My brother is trying to exchange me with a young girl he has wanted to marry for a long time. She is very young, the daughter of an old, nasty, ugly man, with a face covered by chicken pox. His first wife has died and the second is sick and almost bedridden. He wants me to look after his children and house. This idea has been floating around, but I begged my father not to allow it. Last time my brother brought it up, I threatened to kill myself with mouse poison. My father stopped my brother from exchanging me. He didn't talk to me for one month and has been strict with me ever since. But the old man has promised to top his girl up with some money in exchange for me. I think this time my brother has talked my father into the deal. He told me he was old, poor and sick, and could use the money for his treatment. My threats, cries and three-day hunger strike didn't help to change his mind.

There will be no school, no future, no life for me after this. You taught us to have hopes. I was hoping that one day I would be a teacher like you—have my own salary, buy my own clothes and maybe marry a young, educated man of my own choice. All that will turn to ashes in the burning oven of living with the old man. There will be no more school, no more learning and no more books. I am burning my notebooks and with them my hopes and ideals.

Teacher! Forgive me for being frank with you. Maybe you should stop teaching us about hope. You are here for only a few months and tell us about the future, love and justice. You plant the seeds of these ideals in our minds. But our lives are barren meadows of injustice and despair. It is the reality of our lives.

You can't change this. You can't rescue me from this trap. Even if you wanted to, our system doesn't allow you to break the chain of our living realities. Your own father won't permit you. All you can do is to feel sorry for me. Or write about me one day. That's all. So maybe instead you should just teach us how to be patient and suffer. Don't teach us about justice. Tell us how to welcome injustice.

When you read this letter, I may be gone, but please either teach my classmates the skills to hope while suffering, the art to live in death; or don't give them hope.

Your loving student and friend forever,

Hawa

I couldn't wait to go to school the next day and see Hawa, but I didn't know what to tell her. Could I ask her to resist? How? What would the consequences be? Would I be able to face them for her and for me?

When I went to the class the next day, I saw that Hawa was encircled by a group of friends from her class and other classes in the school. She looked pale—awfully pale—and weak. Her lips were bluish and trembling. The girls from other classes left as they saw me. Those in the class sat on their benches. There were whispers. I tried not to be distracted by Hawa and started the class.

Hawa had her head down on the desk. She must have had a sleepless night, I thought, and continued writing on the blackboard.

"Teacher!" the girl sitting next to Hawa shouted. Hawas's head was tilted to one side. Her face was yellow. She looked unconscious. "Teacher! She has poisoned herself," the girl cried.

The principal didn't let me take her to the hospital. It was already too late. Hawa was right. I couldn't do anything.

I didn't attend her funeral. I wasn't allowed, as no woman or girl was ever allowed to attend a funeral in Afghanistan. I didn't even go to her house to participate in *Fateha*—the women prayers—for her. It didn't really matter. I left the school and then, finally, Kunar.

Hawa's letter brought agonizing questions to my mind. Hope or submission? Was it a question of life or death? Or was it the edge between dream and reality? I couldn't give up on hope, even if it was in vain. But her letter left me with many unanswered questions about the lives of women in Kunar. It revealed many new angles and twists in hearing and interpreting the stories of women's love and despair.

Chapter X

Jamila in Blossom

Life in Kunar was full of surprises. Kunar was notorious for its strict tribalism and conservative lifestyle, but the rough mountains and stormy river—its rigid pathways to life—made it unique. In fact, every aspect of life there was unique: it had the only hospital, the only girls' school and the only court, all in the capital. Days were filled with either the boredom of inactive life indoors or the anxiety of perilous adventures and their doomed consequences.

After I quit teaching at the girls' school, my father remained my only contact with life outside our house. In the hot days of summer, we would sit in the balcony facing the open fields and the Kunar river. My dad advised us girls to keep a very low profile and be invisible as much as we could. We, the girls, walked bending so people could not see us from outside. Politicians, especially governors, had to represent and share the traditional values of their citizens. Otherwise, they wouldn't be trusted, they would be considered outsiders. The same was true for my father.

For me, inside the house, life was a safe routine of comfort and luxury. But for the women of Kunar, life floated over the wild waves and echoed through dusty winds of hardship, anguish, hatred and violence. Comfort, hope, love and peace were as rare in their lives as hardship was in ours.

One summer night, I was trying to fall asleep on the balcony after a long, lazy day. The bright blinking stars in the sky seemed to reflect stories of countless nights. The roar of Kunar river below the balcony echoed the cries of the storyteller–women of Kunar, I thought. I heard a knock at the gate. I thought I was imagining sounds. A soldier was guarding the house. Who could it be at that time of the night? I tried to ignore it. The knocks became louder and louder. I clearly heard banging on the door. This was not un-usual; many times there were urgent cases for my father to attend to: a robbery, a murder, a criminal investigation of some kind. I sat on my mat. My father was up. He had gone downstairs and was talking to the guard.

"Sir, there is a woman. A young woman. She is begging to be given refuge in your house. She says people are chasing her to kill her," the guard said.

"Are you sure? A woman begging for protection?" I heard my fa-ther say. By then almost everybody was up: my mother, my father's special guard inside the house, our maid.

I tiptoed downstairs as soon as I heard my father. It always frightened me to see him getting involved in conflicts like that. The woman's deep shaky voice could be heard then: "For God's sake, Mr. Governor! Rescue me!"

As soon as my father heard the woman, he walked toward the

door. I followed him, ignoring my mother's urging to stay in.

The guard asked my father if he should bring the woman in, but my father said no and went out the door himself. I followed. A beautiful, tall, slim young woman in a long green dress and big red shawl was standing at the gate. She had big round eyes. There were small dot tattoos on her forehead, cheeks and chin. She was wearing a round silver nose ring. She held her shoes in one hand and was standing barefoot, her face pale and panicked. As soon as she saw my father, she sat right down at his feet.

"Sir, my name is Jamila. Save my life," said the woman in a shivering, low voice. "I'll be your slave for the rest of my life. I will be your wife's maid until I die. Please don't give me away to those wild animals. They are going to kill me. They are going to cut me to pieces. They are coming. I ran away last night. Please, Governor."

"Who is coming after you? Who is going to kill you? Why? Speak," said my father as he pulled his feet away from her grasp.

"Sir, my husband, Haji, is an old man. He can't be a husband in the way religion and society demand. He is a dying man. His cousins are following me. They want to kill me."

"Why?" my father asked again.

Jamila was silent. Then she took a deep breath and said, "I am a young woman. I have desires. My arms need a baby. My breasts need a baby. My body needs love and warmth. My husband is only good for eating and sleeping. He has fallen asleep on me many times, even when he was much younger.

"Many men desired me. I resisted them all these years. But finally, the other evening, I was deceived by evil and threw myself into the fire of sin with the teacher. He is the only man who talks to me and cares about me. He is the only man who asks how I feel and how I am. They didn't see his face; he ran away. But they saw me. Haji's first wife caught me. She told Haji. He can't do anything himself, but had her call his cousins from another village. They came to avenge Haji's honour."

"You know, Sister, this is a serious family matter," my father responded gravely. "It is about a man's honour and his personal life—I mean a very personal part of his life. I can ask your cousins to forgive you, but I can't keep you with me. They'll kill me if I hide you, you know that. But don't worry, I will take care of your cousins. For now, go and stay in the commander's office. They have an extra room. I will order the guards to give you food and water. Go now."

The next day, when Father came home, the first question my mother asked him was about Jamila.

"Well, actually, she was very right. Her husband's cousins came asking the Commander for 'their honour,' Jamila. I talked to them about right and wrong and a little about the religious law that considers a woman an equal human being to a man. I made them promise not to hurt Jamila. They were polite and agreed, but hinted that if we stood by Jamila or didn't give her away to them, the entire village would rise up against the government," my father said.

The men who came to kill Jamila promised not to harm her and took her back to the village. Not two weeks later, my father told us that Jamila had been killed by the cousins and buried quietly.

The news deeply saddened us. Jamila's story added another blinking star in the sky and a deeper cry to the roars of the Kunar river for me.

It was Jamila's father who came to sue Haji over his daughter's murder. I heard from my father what he heard from Jamila's father.

Jamila's father was a poor man and worked as a hired farmer for the *khan* family, like most of his fellow villagers. His wife died giving birth to his first daughter, but the daughter had survived and he called her Jamila. She needed care and, with the help of a *khan* who lent him his payments in advance, he managed to marry a second wife. From the second wife, he had three children.

Jamila started working hard, and by the time she was five years old she was doing the heavy housework and caring for her half-brothers and -sisters. By the time Jamila was nine, she fetched water, collected wood to feed the fire in the mud stove, prepared dough for her mother to bake the bread for breakfast, swept the yard and fed the animals before everyone else was up. Caring for her baby brothers and sisters was her unquestioned responsibility.

Jamila's father knew his wife was not treating Jamila well, but he couldn't do anything about it. He felt Jamila owed her life to the stepmother. After all, she was the one who breastfed her. Jamila had never known a mother's care and thought it was just what it was, but as she grew older, she began to notice how her stepmother treated her brothers and sister differently. It hurt her father to see

Jamila being mistreated and unloved.

Haji Rahman was one of the people who often talked about Jamila. He was a respected old man who had gone to Mecca for the *Hajj* and thereby acquired the title Haji. He wasn't very well off, but because of his religious position, villagers brought him gifts and even money at times. People would bring their sick children to him for spiritual treatment. Occasionally, he would even be asked to release evil spirits thought to be present in a mentally ill villager. Haji would recite verses from the Quran and then write the verses on a small piece of paper to be folded and attached to the patient's body. In return, the villagers brought him money or food, even a goat or a sheep, now and then. Haji was married, with two wives and many children. He had grown sons and a married daughter, but he was financially able to afford a third wife.

One day, as Haji spoke to Jamila's father, he proposed to marry Jamila. He indicated that Jamila was in the hands of her stepmother and only her father could end her daily hardship by sending her to a husband's house. Haji taunted Jamila's father about her, saying she was at a proper age for marriage, yet remained single. According to Haji, a girl beyond puberty was a burden to her father's house. He said she would be free from her stepmother and her father would be relieved from feeding an extra mouth if she got married. But Haji already had two wives. He promised that his two other wives wouldn't treat Jamila badly.

Haji promised Jamila's father that she would be well fed and secure in his house, but Haji was seventy years old and Jamila was a child. Haji said that it didn't matter for a man, since he was sure

Jamila could have a child from him.

This proposal left Jamila's father dumbstruck. He imagined Jamila as a baby girl asking for his attention. But the reality was bitter and it silenced him. Images of Jamila's long days of hard work under a cruel stepmother flashed through his mind and the thought of having money intrigued him. His conscience bowed under thoughts of gain and loss, love and pain, life and death. Haji married Jamila a month later.

She got her first period in her husband's house and passed through all the other stages of young womanhood under Haji and his two middle-aged wives. Jamila was too young to behave like other brides—she was still a child, happy to play outside and easily made upset or pleased. Losing a game and not having new clothes saddened her more than Haji's criticism or anger.

By the time Jamila was seventeen, her husband had withdrawn from almost every pleasure of life. He had no sexual desire or potency left for Jamila. As she was blossoming into youth, Haji was growing older and weaker. Jamila and Haji were at agonizing extremes: Haji was aging rapidly while Jamila was anxiously exploring her hidden desires. Haji and his two wives could not keep Jamila isolated. She was a normal young woman, full of youth and life.

Haji complained to Jamila's father many times that she arrived home late each time she went to fetch water, that she spoke to other men and liked to socialize with them. If a man happened her way, she didn't really try to avoid him, even though that was the expectation. People started talking about Jamila as a sexy young woman with an old impotent husband. Whatever she did or said was noticed and gossiped about. Before she really understood what was happening, she had a reputation. She was called names: the desiring woman, the sexy widow. Married women became jealous of Jamila. But Jamila seemed unaffected by all the talk and remained a happy, carefree young woman.

My father heard all this from Jamila's father. By then it was too late for her father to keep the secrets or for my father to act upon the story. Jamila's father knew that even if he filed a suit against Haji, and even if the government put him on trial, he couldn't change Jamila's destiny. But he was trying anyway. Even if the government arrested Haji and put him on trial, he would be acquitted on all tribal and traditional accounts and political rationales.

That was how governors resolved cases involving honour, and that was how my father responded to Jamila's pleas for help: by letting loose the frayed ends of her life. He said that neither he nor any other governor would dare intervene in such a personal case—a man's honour, the honour of his family, comes above all else. My father told me how he could not ease his own conscience. He ended up arresting Haji's cousins and putting them in prison.

Jamila's father justified his part by explaining that life had somehow trapped Jamila. He told my father remorsefully, "It is hard to say how she was trapped or who was to blame: her mother for dying too young, me for my lack of vigilance or Haji's greed? Nonetheless, she was trapped and didn't know it."

I was losing perspective instead of gaining it. I wondered if my father was truly upset by Jamila's death or if he was upset because he had been wrong. Or was my father upset that Haji's cousins paid him no mind and killed Jamila anyway, thereby offending the honour of the governor? What about Jamila's father?

"Life" had trapped Jamila as it seemed to trap everybody, men and women alike. But, as far as I was concerned, "life" did not seem to take such an active part—people trapped other people. In my mind, it was more likely that a woman would be trapped or used as bait.

Men? Sometimes they were ensnared within their own traps. Or was it an inertia that consumed all of us? I was ignorant of the truth, if the truth did exist.

Chapter XI

Aday

M y days at home in Kunar may have felt dull and boring for me as I waited to hear when the university would open, but as I heard people's stories, I realized that life there had no certainty. The few stories that made their way to the government and the governor's ear were enough to reveal how people lived in Kunar.

Aday's story was one of those few that reached the office of the governor, my father. It stunned him, and equally shocked me, when he shared it with us.

> This morning when I was going to my office, I saw Aday, an older woman around her sixties with a bulky bag across her shoulders, standing at the door. She looked exhausted and miserable, with red, tired eyes and a haggard face.
>
> "What is the matter, my good mother?" I asked.
>
> "I need justice, your honour. Justice! For God's sake, if you don't listen in this world, I'll take my appeal to God in the world after," she blasted.

I was shaken by such an outburst from an old woman and asked her to come in the office to talk. The guard was trying to push her back, but I nodded to let her pass.

I was hardly settled in my chair when Aday began to untie the knots, one by one, from the top of the big bag she was carrying on her shoulders. She became hysterical. Her whole body shook. Then, with an angry shriek that sounded more like a cry, she raised the bloody, bruised head of a dead female and started shaking it towards me.

Half crying, half talking, she said, "This is my daughter. They killed my daughter. They hit her with an axe in the light of day. No fear of God. No fear of justice. No fear of my wounded heart. They just did it."

Aday moaned and slumped over the bag, slowly removing piece after piece of her daughter's body to show us. I couldn't stand it anymore and yelled at her to stop. I told her it was a sin to do that to her daughter's body. I probably looked very shaken, as my secretary came in and pulled the old woman back from the bag and shoved it aside. I sent for the judge and the security officer to come and hear her story.

I was numb hearing my father tell us this horrible story, but I wasn't shocked. It was another version of Hawa and Jamila's stories.

It, too, reflected the colours of poison and blood, and echoed the same cries of crushed hopes and condemned love.

Father told us the whole story later. Aday, sitting in front of the governor, the judge and the security chief, holding on to a bag full of the remains of her slaughtered daughter, had told this story:

I begged my son not to bargain her away, but he didn't listen. He didn't hear his sister's cries, either. He made the deal and gave my daughter in exchange for the other man's young sister, who was still a child. My son's bride came to my house and my beautiful daughter went to another woman's house. Yes, this mad pig had a wife and children; he didn't need another wife at all. I thought he wanted another wife because he did not get sons from the first one, which is the only good reason for a man to want a second wife. But this man never treated my child any better than his first wife. Not even a year passed before he started to beat my daughter. She was beaten for laughing, for speaking out of turn, for coming to visit me and staying an hour later than he had asked her. God knows what else. He wasn't the man for my beautiful, cheerful girl.

The day this most horrible of human sins took place, I was not home. I was in the city. When I came home, I saw my daughter in small pieces. She was an innocent child, without fault and in no way deserving of this fate. On this day, they told me her husband was working in the fields. He usually worked until late afternoon, but that morning he had come back earlier. When he came into the backyard, he saw my daughter, his wife, handing a glass of water to one of the labourers inside their big *qala*. Everyone in the village knew my daughter to have a smiling face. She was friendly with the elderly, with the young and with adults. She wasn't loose; she was a happy and kind person.

Perhaps she smiled at the labourer when she handed him a glass of water. Her husband must have seen it. He went straight to his room and told his first wife that he was not a man to tolerate his wives flirting with other men. He took his gun, loaded it, put it inside his vest pocket and walked outside to face the labourer. His first wife said that less than a minute later she heard shots and then the sound of a body collapsing. When she rushed outside, she saw the labourer and my daughter on the ground, soaked in blood. People began to gather. My daughter's brothers-in-law, both of them, came and circled the dead.

My daughter's husband proudly announced that he had killed his wife because he caught her flirting with the labourer. The men in our village thought this was a way of preserving their honour. They took the murderer's side. He then cut my daughter to pieces, claiming he did it to keep the family honour and reputation from stain. Nobody said anything. The men kept quiet and admired his bravery and honour. Even my son was silent; he said it was a matter of honour.

The labourer's brother came from the next village and took the body away in shame and guilt. He apologized to the family for his brother's violation of their honour. Maybe he didn't know his own brother, but I knew my child. I am sure she wasn't flirting with that man. For God's sake! Wouldn't you give a glass of water to a thirsty stranger?

I swear to God my daughter was innocent. I want you to punish my son-in-law. I want him in jail. Otherwise, my heart will burn in anger. I don't care what the village men would say. Of course, they would say it was for Hashem Khan's honour and he deserved to defend it and nobody should interfere. But I claim my daughter didn't offend his honour. If you take Hashem Khan's side, I will go to the capital and appeal for justice there. I will say you took the side of injustice.

My father said he listened to Aday's story patiently and was agonized with sympathy and anger. There was no doubt in his mind that he should side with Aday, but in such a delicate case where a man's honour was at stake, he had to be political. He said that when it came to issues of honour, their policy assumed non-interference, even if it was a clear case of murder.

In that part of the country, Kunar Province, tribal family law normally dictated the code of justice. In rural areas, they are strict about observing traditional codes of honour, called *Pashtunwali*. Land, wife, daughter and sister are all part of the family honour. Honour killing rarely, if ever, subjects the murderer to justice. It is simply not considered a crime to murder in order to protect family honour.

So, Aday's valiant and anguished demand for justice for her daughter failed. All it prompted was a heavy silence from the government. They, according to my father, didn't have much to say to Aday, except for a few words of condolence. But Father said he asked Aday to file a lawsuit against her son-in-law, Hashem Khan. They had all requested that she bury the remains of her daughter, but she refused until they had an answer for her.

Father's office was next to our residence. It was a compound built around orchards and gardens. From our upstairs window, we could see the front yard of Father's office, where people waited to see him or brought papers for signing. There was always a crowd of men wandering or sitting under the trees there, and sometimes a few women, too.

After my father told us Aday's story, I tried to spot her among the crowd. The very next afternoon, I saw a woman leaning against the trunk of a tree with a big load by her side. We had binoculars that we used to look at the mountains and animals in the faraway fields. With the binoculars, the scene was clear. An older woman was sitting, wearing a long black shawl—customary for married and older *Pashtun* women—wrapped around her knees and over her hands. She was staring at the security guard walking around the garden. I was sure it was Aday.

I asked the guard at the door to bring her in. He said it was my father's order not to treat any of the clients differently; it would be considered a favour to Aday to come to the governor's house and speak to his daughter. But I insisted and the guard finally let her in.

Aday came inside, but sat by the gate. She looked worn out. The blue tattoos on her forehead had faded away between her wrinkles. Her long face, narrow chin and dark, deep eyes made her look thin. She had a loose, dark, dotted blue dress down to her calves, and black baggy pants. A painted red scarf was tied around her waist like a cumberbund. She was not wearing shoes, and her feet looked cracked and hardened with dirt and dust.

"God! I am dying of thirst. Get me some water, daughter, will you?" she asked, looking straight into my eyes.

I didn't want to leave her side, so I signaled to my younger sister to bring water. Aday was looking around, trying to settle into a comfortable sitting position.

"Are you his daughter?" she asked me.

"The governor? Yes," I answered.

"You think he will avenge my daughter's blood?" Aday asked.

"I don't know, dear Aday! He doesn't tell us about his official work. But tell me, how did you come here and from where?" I asked. My father was very strict about keeping his family away from his work and forbade us from making promises or doing favours for anyone.

Aday looked me up and down with suspicion, but didn't say anything. Her hand was searching for something around the waist of her loose dress. She took her hand out with a round metal container of mouth tobacco. She put some green crushed tobacco in her palm, stirred it with her finger and threw it into her mouth with a backward jerk of her head. She was relaxing, it seemed.

Aday started to loosen up, keeping the tobacco under her tongue. "Daughter! I have come a long way. From the village of Wooden Bridge. I have walked three days and three nights." Aday was pointing her three fingers repeatedly.

"How did you come? By bus? Horse? Donkey?" I asked, curious to hear.

Tapping on her bare feet, Aday said, "On foot! On foot! One pair of shoes is used up. Most of the way I walked barefoot. Barefoot. Do you know? Barefoot!" Aday was shaking her head when she said that.

"Where did you spend the nights, mother? Weren't you scared?" I asked.

She pulled her big black shawl up from around her waist and took a big butcher knife from under her red waistband. Without a word, Aday held up the knife and put it back.

"But where did you sleep?" my younger sister asked.

Aday looked amused and sighed, "What do you know? You rich city girls? Do you really want to know how I came and why I came? Do you have the patience for my story?" Aday asked.

Before we could say anything, she sat up, facing us, and gave us the details of her three day trip to the city:

> I walked long distances during the day, stopping only for short breaks to chuck some dried fruit into my mouth. Nights I spent at the local mosques. Some *Mullahs* and their *Talib* were nice and shared their food with me; some didn't or didn't have enough. In any case, they gave me a spot to lay my head down and rest for a few hours. I lay on a mat in the corner of the big room, pulled the heavy bag into an embrace, drew my shawl around my body and closed my eyes for a night's sleep.
>
> Three days later, when I reached here, at the governor's office, the guards told me that the offices were closed until the next day. I just went and sat on the ground with the other people waiting to see an officer in charge. I laid my belongings in front of me, put my head on my knees and waited to see the governor the next day.

Aday spat the tobacco out, pointed to the guard who was standing with his back toward us and continued.

These soldiers, these guards, whatever you call them, they teased me; asked unseemly questions, told dirty jokes in front of me. They didn't even offer me a glass of water. But I kept quiet, and waited and waited and waited. Until your father came. They wouldn't let me see him; they were pushing me back, but I just pushed them away and met your father. He is a good man; not a bad man at all. God bless him! He let me in and listened to me. Did he tell you what the bastards did to my daughter?

Aday asked this with a piercing stare at me. The question, the story of her daughter and the sight of the bag by her side gave me a chill.

Hurriedly, I said, "Oh, yes, I am sorry." But fearing she would open the bag or say more about her daughter's murder, I quickly asked, "So what are you doing now? What is your next step?"

Aday turned her face to the gate, pointing to the officers, and said:

I don't know, daughter. The governor said I should file a suit against my coward son-in-law. A guy in the office helped and took me to one of those people who write this sort of letter. I took that back to the judge's office. Now I am waiting to hear what they do. If they arrest my daughter's murderers, I will rest in peace. If not, what else can I do? If they don't avenge my daughter's murder for me in this world, I will pray God will show them how bitter it feels.

The next day, I heard from Father that they had consoled Aday, convinced her to bury her daughter's remains here at the cemetery and go back to her village while her case was investigated.

I thought of Aday for many days. How would she have felt burying the remains of her daughter in a strange and remote place, away from her village? How long would she wait to hear about her file? Would she ever hear about it? How would she treat her daughter-in-law, the sister of her daughter's murderer?

I had heard about many similar cases where unresolved bitterness victimized the innocent exchanged bride. Would Aday turn bitter towards her own daughter-in-law and take her anger out on her? Wouldn't the bitterness poison her? Would it matter at all?

Then later, as a young woman, I thought about the story of Aday and wondered about bitterness, revenge and honour. The concepts of "justice," "injustice," "victim," and "oppressor" had become real faces and real people.

CHAPTER XII

Frozen Memories, Frozen Times

I went to university and started studying at the faculty of languages and literature. Our philosophy professor was new. Dr. Shahir had just returned from Germany with a PhD. I fell in love with him the first day he gave a lecture to us. He talked with passion about Bertolt Brecht, the German modern playwright, and had translated his work into Pashto. As crazy as I was about literature, I clung to this name and whatever I heard from Dr. Shahir about him. I was probably trying to create a connection.

Shahir was a philosopher, understood psychology and wanted to publish. I was striving to be a writer and was writing short stories. We both had intellectual agendas, but he was learned and I was just a beginner.

I saw Dr. Shahir every day. Days that he didn't lecture, I would find a question to take to his office. By the time I heard about his personal life and the fact that he was married with two children, I was already deeply in love with him. My attempts to deny my feelings and acknowledge another woman's life with him were in vain. I was stuck.

But I was torn apart inside and still pretending the relationship was a simple friendship between a much older professor and a young student. He was forty years old and I was twenty-three when, one day, Dr. Shahir made me admit my true feelings and give up the surface pretension. He said, "Don't try to deny it, but you are deeply in love with me."

I couldn't resist such a bold confrontation. I became involved with a married man almost twice my age. Then, with guilt and regret, I was deeply involved. I had this inner debate that I was stealing another woman's man, but we continued with sneaky dates in his car, and I would talk about my guilt and try to justify our affair and deeper involvement. He said that if I left him, he would find someone else; I made him a happier husband and father.

Our love was a secret with many layers, hidden from my family, from his wife, from society and from my conscience. Dating was more dangerous than robbery. I could see him in my house, as a family guest, or in his office, formally, but dating was almost impossible. I was taking an English class in the evening. He would pick me up and drop me home in half an hour. I then told my parents that I had taken a bus. That half an hour in the car was our private life, and on those nights there was not a single moment that I spent with him when I wasn't also thinking about his wife. I never forgave myself for being in love with him. But I also never stopped loving him.

As much as I loved Shahir, I was determined to get my higher education abroad. I wanted to become a professional writer and get my master's degree in literature. Shahir supported me wholeheartedly. He used his connections in the government to help me get a passport. By then, my family knew that I was determined to leave for a good cause.

My father did not oppose my decision to go abroad; rather, he showed support and concern. He left me on my own to pay for my travel expenses. Later, I realized he was trying to boost my confidence and make me feel self-sufficient. My mother was also a great supporter of my plans for higher education. Although she didn't have any education herself, she wanted it for her children—especially her daughters. I knew she felt proud of me and put her emotions aside when it came to my education.

Years passed before she told me that my father had actually been quite wary about my traveling alone on the long journey from Kabul to New York. But with my own professional connections, my brother in the United States, Shahir's help and family support, I finally got a passport to go to the States to study. My brother and his wife being in Iowa made it easier; he told me to just get my tuition and he would provide the rest.

It was April, 1978. I got ready to fly to New York and then to Iowa City to join my brother. Just before I was about to leave for America, I went to say goodbye to my relatives.

One day, while I was in the village, we continuously heard military music on the radio instead of the regular programs. It went on for hours. Some men went to the city to find out what was happening. They came back with the news of a coup d'état. Aslam Watanjar, the minister of defence, had seized control of the army and ousted President Daoud from power. The Communist Party leaders who were in prison and supposed to be executed the next day took power and declared a communist government.

It took the entire nation by surprise. Among the many political parties that had grown under our democracy, three were well organized and established: The Parcham and Khalq parties held similar socialist views and were both influenced by the Toda party of Iran, while the third party, Shola, represented Maoist ideology. About ten days before the coup d'état, one of the prominent leaders of Parcham had been killed while the Parcham and Khalq parties negotiated forming an alliance. His funeral drew thousands of students and intellectuals into the street and made an embarrassing scene for the government, which was blamed for the conspiracy of his murder. The government put all of the Parcham leaders in prison with plans to execute them.

We heard one of the Communist leaders giving a speech on the radio, saying that the cruel Sardar Daoud had been thrown out and replaced by the Communists.

I left for America ten days later, and there I heard the rest of the stories about the Communist regime and their atrocities. I heard that they were arresting each and every person who said something about the government or even mentioned the leaders' names casually. Doctors, engineers, professors, writers, poets, students—all were targeted and lived in fear of being the next one dragged away from their homes in the middle of the night.

Shahir was a free-thinking philosopher, a frank and friendly person, witty and knowledgeable. He would not stop telling stories or jokes for any consideration of offending his friends. He spoke freely, openly criticized the government, the system and the Russians. Khad, the intelligence service at that time, was everywhere; it penetrated families, among friends, in schools and in offices. Everyone was invited to report to the Khad: young boys and girls; older men and women; whoever was too naive, too shrewd or even too loose. Many street boys who were bullies were employed as Khad servicemen.

The Communists took the whole nation hostage. Shahir, like most other intellectuals, had a socialist outlook; he desired social justice and resented racial, class-based and gender discrimination. The Communists, however, played dirty political tricks with these socialist ideologies: they claimed justice for the poor, but in practice further oppressed them. The Communists forced land reform and took land from the *khans*, but by never giving any land to the poor, this only provoked them.

With the corruption in the system and people's resentment of their laws, these laws couldn't be implemented. But they created chaos. The rich found a way around it, but the poor lost whatever they had. By bombarding the villages to kill one or two *Mujahid*, they hurt the landlords who had solid buildings and basements, but destroyed the mud and thatch homes of poor farmers. Compulsory military service for men and boys over eighteen only dragged those from families who didn't have the connections and money to bribe the authorities. Many village boys were forced to fight against their own people or sent to war fronts while the sons of the rich and elite relied upon their connections and money to obtain exemption from military service.

Thousands of villagers and poor families lost their only sons, often the only literate people in their neighborhoods. Many never heard from their sons again, many received the news of their martyrdom years after they were dead and many more were asked to go to the military hospital and look for their sons among rows and rows of coffins with pieces of shattered bodies. Never was a rich or powerful father given such a test. The boys in those coffins were usually the only breadwinners, sons of old widows or peasant fathers who weren't living in the city and had no place to go.

Between 1978 and 1984, those first years of Soviet-backed Communist power in Afghanistan, the villages were bombed, the towns were ruined, the fields and gardens burned. Millions of people who lost their homes, land and properties fled the country, going to neighbouring Pakistan or Iran to become refugees.

Communism brought with it death, destruction, torture and a bitterness that pervaded all aspects of life. Communism was, in fact, a culture that did not believe in God. For Afghan Muslims, whether practicing or not, God is present from birth to death. Nothing could be more cruel and alien than a culture devoid of God. What brought this curse to the country was a question that disturbed the mind of every Afghan; they sought reasons behind their own beliefs. Some blamed the previous system for conditions that led to communism while some misogynists blamed the immodesty of modern Afghan women as the reason for God's anger. Some even blamed democracy for letting the leftist parties exist.

Other governments jumped in, each with a political motivation. The Americans, the Saudis and the Pakistanis all supported the freedom fighters called *Mujahideen*. The intellectuals—who had believed in socialist ideology and were known as leftist radicals—became quickly disillusioned and only for survival reasons continued their jobs as professors or doctors within the government.

The government silenced the people. Kabul was turned upside down by the scarcity of logic and justice, and the inflation of brutality and corruption of narrow-minded politicians. One-by-one, professionals and intellectuals were kidnapped from their homes in the middle of the night on charges of dissent against the government.

This became a series of nightmares that darkened the lives of every civilian. It didn't take much for the government to destroy a family and a life. The government Jeeps would stop at the door of a targeted individual. A few Khad agents would take the person with them and drive away through the night. The families would then try in vain to trace some sign of their missing family member in prisons and bases.

Shahir was a victim of these raids. I heard that on one night, well past midnight, a Jeep stopped at his house and the men banged on the door loudly and persistently. He had but a moment to reach for his gown to cover his pyjamas and answer the door. This was the last time Shahir saw his wife, sick mother and dear children. There was no sign of him after that. Nobody would give the family any information, though it was understood that he was in jail.

I often wonder what happened to him and whether his broken soul is somehow still connected to this world. Nobody heard anything more of his life or death after he was taken away, except that someone saw him in the prison one day, when he was brought back from torture. It was said that his face was swollen and bruised. He had told the person to tell his friends to be careful.

After Shahir disappeared, his brothers tried to make connections in the government to locate him. His wife waited at home. His young son went to the neighbour's house and said he would not come home until his father returned. His mother was old and sick, but went to the main prison, *Pul-e-Charkhi*, every weekend for a year. Eventually, her energy completely drained and she gave up. The rest of his family did not give up hope. The last time I was in Kabul, I heard that Shahir's wife still got upset when anyone considered her husband dead.

Shahir's family was not alone. There were many other wives, mothers and children who went to *Pul-e-Charkhi* in Kabul every weekend hoping to see their loved ones. The visitors would wait behind the steel gate to hear something from the guards. Visitors usually brought clothing or food for their relatives. Sometimes, when the guards took the things inside, the visitors saw it as a sign of their loved ones being there. But when the clothing or food was rejected, it usually meant that he was no longer there, he'd either been killed or transferred to another prison.

The last I heard from Shahir's wife was that she is still waiting to hear from him. His mother died in despair.

I also heard rumours that many prisoners were taken away in the night to a remote, isolated area. They were told to dig a very big hole. Then, they were told to jump into it. Then the guards drove bulldozers on top of them to smooth the land. The prisoners were buried alive. People in Kabul say that they could hear the shrieking and screaming of the prisoners as the bulldozers rolled over them.

In 1984, when I went home to visit my family and to see and feel my country again, I heard many stories like this.

Chapter XIII

Foreign Student, Foreign Land

In 1984, I had finished my course work for getting a PhD in education at the University of Illinois and I decided to go back to Afghanistan to collect data for my dissertation on the dual role of work and household for women. In those days, this was a hot topic in Women's Studies. Private and public domain and the dichotomy of roles were discussed in books. Afghan women in Kabul were in public jobs with full recognition at that time, however, unlike today, their lives were unexplored. A PhD was my last academic goal to achieve. By then, I had lived in the US for six years and had completed two master's degree programs.

I first came to the United States in May, 1978, and joined my brother in Iowa City, where I soon realized that I wasn't really on my own. My brother didn't interfere with my work, my studies or my social life at all. My sister-in-law was like a real, kind sister and took care of me well. In a way, it felt like home. I was supported and protected. I liked that, but I also yearned for a much wider space and time to be left on my own and find my way by myself. I also wanted to be in a bigger university with more international students. For these reasons, I decided to transfer to the University of Illinois at Urbana-Champaign.

My brother drove me to Champaign. We checked into a motel outside the city and he left early in the morning the next day. Then, I was really by myself to find my way in this unknown city. I had five hundred dollars, a letter for tuition and a fee waiver. I rented a room in a student house right by the main road on campus for a hundred and twenty dollars. Finding a job was the next step, and in the meantime I budgeted myself to a maximum of ten dollars per week for food and everything else. How I managed is a different story. Ready-made macaroni and cheese packages were my main meals. At the time, I didn't think it was a hardship, but now I remember how my knees felt weak from hunger when I walked up and down the stairs in the library.

I was young and considered exotic since there were not many Afghans in the United States. I was the only Afghan student at the university and there was only one Afghan professor, who was married to an American. Those six years added a different layer of marginality to my life. I had much more freedom than in Afghanistan: I was free to choose my friends, my social life and my lifestyle. I was treated well, even special, for being an Afghan and an outgoing woman. At first I struggled with the language, but soon got the hang of it and was fine. I had very good friends. I was working hard to earn my living—usually two jobs—cleaning bottles and strangely shaped glass containers in a chemistry lab, and working in the library. Later, I got a scholarship.

Yet there was something missing in my life, or maybe something was always added. I don't know how many times I heard the question, "Where are you from?" I didn't know then, but now I find myself avoiding it. There was no discrimination or ethnocentrism, at least at the university; I felt wholly part of the school and the community. But, I was a foreign student.

Champaign was a university town. The university library was one of the best in the nation. It was there where I spent my days and nights. Those six years—one in Iowa and five in Champaign—are associated with the long halls of the library, different subjects on different floors, and my desk on the top floor among the stacks of shelves. I spent most of my time there, usually leaving my desk only when I heard the bell ring for closing at two in the morning.

Every night when I rode my bike home, I promised myself that I would not do it again, as rape was the only terror I allowed to scare me. That was more or less my life; I was growing intellectually out of Muslim women's inhibitions and learning to claim, or reclaim, myself. It was during this time that I learned how we had been taught to disown our bodies. In theory, I changed. In reality, however, I remained confined to the sexual identity of restraint. I immersed myself in my studies and suppressed my social and sexual life completely.

I first earned an MA in Comparative Literature. Although I had planned to return to Afghanistan, the situation there was not right for me to go back. By then I also had personal and academic connections that made me interested in studying more social issues relating to women, development and education. So I enrolled in an educational policy program and chose to study women in development as my minor.

Still holding on to my dream of becoming a professor in Kabul, I prolonged my studies and enrolled in a Masters of Education program. By the time I completed the course work and wrote my thesis, the situation in Afghanistan was even worse. I then decided to work towards a PhD. This uncertainty about my country and my future made it impossible for me to celebrate completion and achievement. I remember how, from my tenth grade in school, I had thought, spoken and dreamed about getting a master's degree. Even my mother, who was illiterate herself, shared the dream with me. But when I actually received the degree, it felt as though I were just running another errand.

That afternoon, I was hurrying to a course for my second MA program when I remembered that I had to pick up my first MA diploma from the basement of the administration building. I rushed down, signed a paper and the clerk said, "Congratulations, Sharifa Sharif." I said thank you and ran to my class. I didn't have time to celebrate, but for a short moment I thought about my mother, my dreams and my life, and my chest grew heavy. That was it.

The second degree, in education policy, was similar. At the point of writing my dissertation, however, I was different. The hope for a free Afghanistan was fading away and with it my plan to return for good, but I was completely immersed in academic goals, women's issues and feminism. I thought of Afghanistan as a unique field of study for an original subject. Of course, I also had personal reasons for wanting to see my family, especially my father, who I thought didn't have very long to live.

Afghanistan was in the news every day. I felt history was being made in my country and I shouldn't just read or hear about it, I should feel it. When I heard about the *Mujahideen*—the freedom fighters—part of me was ashamed. I felt bad that I wasn't part of the fight for freedom, but I needed firsthand knowledge and to live through it to fight against it or for it. Part of me hoped that by going to Afghanistan and seeing the cruelty of the Communists and the cause of *Mujahideen*, I would be able to join the fight against the government. I even envisioned joining the guerilla fighters in the mountains.

My PhD advisor, the late Dr. Alan Peshkin, whom I loved and respected wholeheartedly, didn't like my decision to go back to Afghanistan and neither did my friends or my brother. But I decided to go, collect my data and see how I could become part of the struggle.

I returned to Afghanistan in July, 1984, a time when many people were desperate to get out of the country. Nobody thought I should visit at that time, but I went anyway. I witnessed the ruins of the country I had left many years earlier, ruins in every home and every soul. Destroyed buildings, smashed schools, crushed roads, broken homes, vanished people and broken hearts—all told stories filled with death and loss. My country and its people were shattered.

The stories I heard did not fall into any particular sequence, because there was no sequence, no order. People lived their lives in a vacuum. A mother's only son was dragged from his home and brutally murdered for no apparent reason. Fathers disappeared into unknown prisons. Husbands vanished and young wives despaired.

My uncle's young son, Karim, was killed while teaching at a girls' school. Two years later, the grief had hardly subsided when a stranger knocked on my uncle's door and asked him to go to the city at once. As my uncle later told us, his first thought was that his younger son, Aziz, was not well. My uncle jumped into the strange man's Jeep to go to the city. All he could think about was Karim. Then he didn't know who he was thinking about. What had happened?

My uncle reached the hospital in confused silence. Nobody had to tell him that Aziz was unwell; he was smashed to pieces, beyond recognition. My uncle said that he had known this feeling before. Aziz's covered body lay among dozens of others in the basement of the hospital. Uncle was on his own to search for his son's body, to try to identify him by his watch or by the feel of his skin. How he would feel later, how he would take the body of a second son to his mother was of no consequence.

I went to Aziz's funeral. It was an explosion of sorrow and tears, which flowed in no particular direction. Who cried for whom was not important; the grief was all-consuming, shapeless and name-less, it was everywhere.

A young woman seemed to be laughing between sobs. Strong and tall with a thick, full mouth and wide forehead, her big dark eyes shone brightly with tears. She was nineteen years old. I heard a whisper that she was a widow; that caught my attention. Something connected us.

She told me her story: "My parents married me off to a man. He was a few years younger than me. He was a *Mujahid*. I knew he wasn't a family man, but my father feared what might happen if we refused his proposal. Perhaps we would be robbed or killed. I was married to him three years ago, when I was sixteen. He stayed two days and then went to the mountains to join the others. He came home now and then. The last time he came was two and a half years ago. I haven't seen him since. My father has inquired about him but nobody knows anything. I don't know if he's been killed or has gone somewhere else."

The young woman paused for a moment. She still wasn't sure whether or not to open up to me. I wasn't a close friend or family member, but I was a woman and perhaps that was what sufficed as a bond.

"I don't know what to do," she continued. "You are not married, but you are a woman. What do I do?" She attempted to share more, but deferred to the cloak of modest shyness learned by Afghan women.

Women in Afghanistan generally marry once. Marrying a second time is not common and those who do are remarried to their in-laws, a younger brother-in-law or cousin from the father's side. This woman was now living with her own father, which was considered a burden to him. She visited the *Mullah* to ask whether it is Islamic to remarry.

The *Mullah* told her that according to Islamic *Sharia*, since her husband had disappeared and she didn't know for sure if he was dead, she had to wait for him for ninety years. After ninety years, she could remarry. To the *Mullah* it was irrelevant that she would then be 109 years old.

Many young women served their time. Some might have been married off to a younger brother-in-law, like Aziz's young wife, who got married to a brother-in-law ten years her junior. But most young widows waited dutifully. Whether that young woman from the funeral waited to hear from her husband, got married to her brother-in-law or got killed in some random explosion, I don't know. I don't even know her name. I didn't ask. Names didn't matter; stories did.

Chapter XIV

The Aftermath

Disillusioned, after four years in Kabul I abandoned my dreams to join the struggle against the government. The disheartening stories that circulated and tragedies I witnessed left no doubt that the regime was impenetrable. Plentiful were stories of atrocities and betrayals the *Mujahideen* perpetrated upon poor villagers. The villagers were caught between two sides of the fight and both forces terrorized mercilessly. By 1988, the *Mujahideen* had divided into seven groups, each in control of a geographically defined zone; citizens caught in between were forced to choose one group to support. By day, the government and Russians would attack and kill villagers, rape girls and women, torture men. By night, the *Mujahideen* would barge into homes. Seven or eight men would bang on the door demanding good food, then they would spend the night and steal whatever provisions and valuables a household held. It was *sadaqa* for the holy war, they claimed. Many families were obliged to relinquish a young daughter. If a *Mujahid* asked to marry a girl, the family had two choices: give the girl or be killed.

My uncle was one of these victims. While his older sons and daughters studied at faraway city schools, he, his wife and two younger daughters, ages fifteen and sixteen, remained in the village. The girls were not in school. One day, a *Mujahid* commander from *Hezb-e-Islami* asked my uncle for his sixteen-year-old daughter. My uncle had no choice. Discretely, my cousin was married to the twenty-seven-year-old commander. She cried a lot, saying she didn't want to marry a bearded *Mujahid*. But, it was rationalized, at least she was married to a commander.

Her husband didn't turn out to be a bad man. Apart from being fanatically strict about her social life and interactions with men, my cousin would say he was a good husband—she was allowed to go to her father's house with permission, as long as she didn't socialize with men other than her father and brothers. Her husband was killed two years after they married. At eighteen my cousin was forced to marry her brother-in-law, who was then only fifteen. Her in-laws were of the *Pashtun* tribe and *Pashtuns* generally don't permit their widows to marry outside the family; it is considered part of tribal honour to maintain heritage.

I collected stories of various *Mujahid* groups killing innocent people simply because they couldn't recite verses from the Quran, or because an individual looked Western or couldn't pray convincingly enough on the spot. Travelling outside Kabul was always risky for men because whether *Mujahideen* or another militia controlled the region, soldiers would stop vehicles for inspection and board buses to examine the passengers. Several suspects would be chosen and ordered off the bus; very few returned alive and those who did bore horrible stories of torture. Many were skinned alive, then beaten to death. Other victims were conscripted to work in the government.

In Kabul and other Afghan cities, in broad daylight, hostages were taken by the government. At night, outside the cities, groups of *Mujahideen* enacted a similar reign of terror.

It was impossible for me to join the freedom fighters. Each of the many splinter groups had its own extreme nationalist agenda and was motivated by greed and prejudice, resulting in cruelty. Even compared to the government, each group lacked ethical standards. The Communists and Russians slaughtered people in the name of one godless, atheist ideology while the *Mujahideen* did so in the name of a God. The poor, the innocent, men, women, children and families were killed on both fronts. Reluctant soldiers and naive Muslim boys from the mountains were drafted and killed while powerful leaders grew richer on both sides. The ideological dichotomy coupled with the nationalistic hypocrisy of it all left me with no side to take.

Leaving Afghanistan again to go anywhere, the United States especially, was a farfetched idea, an almost impossible task. But I was determined to leave and finish my PhD in Illinois.

Chapter XV

At the Mercy of Refuge

Through my connections in the United Nations, I secured a scholarship to a nine-month program at the International Management Institute in New Delhi. Apart from Eastern Europe, India was the only country to which Afghans could emigrate with a medical or business passport. At that time, the government was sending many young students to Eastern European countries and the Soviet Union, but ordinary people could not get a passport— least of all to Western countries.

To obtain a medical passport, an individual had to prove their illness could not be treated in Afghanistan. It wasn't easy to negotiate, but it was possible with connections and bribes. People lacking money and connections went to Pakistan on foot, by donkey or horse, car or truck. From India and Pakistan, people could then apply for refugee status to Western countries; Canada was a welcoming country for Afghan refugees at the time.

One of my brothers fled to Pakistan and from there was smuggled to Canada. My younger brother studied in East Germany, in reality to escape compulsory military service. My eldest brother remained in the United States. Shortly after my departure to India, my parents and remaining siblings decided to leave Afghanistan, as well. My parents obtained a medical passport—my mother as the patient and my father as her companion. They joined me in India three months later. My brothers who were of draft age could not obtain a passport, so they escaped to Pakistan. We all waited in different countries, hoping eventually to be sponsored to Canada.

For two years, my parents, my younger sister and I suffered in agony as refugees in India. In New Delhi we lived in the servants' quarters of an Indian household. We paid rent and reoriented ourselves from our former life in a house with ten bedrooms, a Mercedes and several servants, to a life of relative poverty with one room for my parents, and a garage for my sister and me. Uncertainty and anxiety engulfed us in India. Our destiny was a dream in the hands of the Canadian or American immigration officers whose approval or disapproval of our applications determined our fate. We, the refugees, had no control in shaping our future outside of India. To buoy faith, refugees depended on superstitions and religion; *Mullahs*, Indian fortunetellers and palm readers became wellsprings of hope.

With my brother's sponsorship, we applied for immigration status to Canada and waited for a letter from the embassy. Before being invited for an embassy interview, we were subject to a medical examination. In the interview, the immigration officer would either accept or reject our petition for family reunion.

Months passed. No news came. One day, I asked another Afghan refugee what I might do to make the medical exams take place sooner.

She took a deep breath. "You know there is a shrine in Old Delhi?" she said sincerely. "Go there four Wednesdays in a row and give alms to the attendants. You will get your medical." Her naïveté stunned me, but so did our helplessness and vulnerability.

A year later, we still had not been summoned for our medical exam and life had become a daily trial. My mother, sister and I went to the shrine. I don't know if I went there for my medical papers or for a sense of security and hope, but it simply felt good and made the days go by faster.

We finally received our medical examination letter. The doctor reported that my father's chest X-ray had revealed a scar. I was upset for my father's health and for our case, but soon others told me a scar was routine code: the doctors sought graft. Bribery was a shame for me; I hesitated before bribing the doctor. Cash, to me, was and still is a mean, not a value. The long bus drive from home to the doctor's office that evening in New Delhi was the most dreadful ride ever. The entire trip, I rehearsed my words to offer him cash. I was to grant the man two hundred dollars, together with quality goods and dried fruit. Most difficult for me was the moment I politely informed the doctor I had a gift for him. He liked it. The next X-ray was clear.

I found a job in one of the United Nations High Commission for Refugees (UNHCR) centres as an English teacher. There I encountered refugees replete with stories. One young man who was never attentive in class and was absent most of the time had lost his wife and three children in a government bombing. He had been out shopping when he heard an explosion in his neighbourhood. He rushed home to find only the ruins of his house and pieces of his family scattered under the debris. He told me he was not capable of concentrating in class and was coming just to pass time.

Another young man could not ease his conscience as he had left an elderly mother behind. Forced to flee the country to Pakistan on foot, he had no way to bring her along.

I witnessed some Afghans who falsely reported about one another; everyone was desperate to abandon India and to establish a solid life in the West. They viewed anyone else in line as the enemy, a rival who could whisk away their only chance of departure to freedom and renewal.

I was shocked when a young lady informed the office that her mother's case was fake—everybody waited for sponsorship to Canada, the United States or Germany; everybody camouflaged their cases and their plans; people left without bidding goodbye to friends; no one indulged in the risk of trust. The office of the UNHCR fed the mistrust by listening to reports and checking on people's domestic situations. The UNHCR gave allowances to families. Eligible families were poor and desperate. Unannounced visits by UNHCR officers to the refugee's home were required in order to assess a family's need based upon their living conditions. A television, good furniture or good food in the house instantly disqualified the family. An officer once told me about an ex-professor that had applied for an allowance.

"This guy is not eligible," he exclaimed. "He served me very expensive biscuits. If he can afford that, he shouldn't be getting help from us."

I felt sick when I heard that. I explained to him that Afghans borrow money to buy sweets to serve with tea to their guests—hospitality is a family's honour and anyone who goes to an Afghan house is a guest. Of course, there were some rich people who stowed their carpets and leather furniture away in anticipation of the UNHCR visit.

A future in Canada seemed too remote. Amidst the miasma of mistrust and disbelief, I, too, lost trust in myself. Day by day, as I experienced the helplessness of not knowing my future, I lost confidence in my ability to stand on my feet and work. Although I had a full life, a respected job and reasonable pay—two thousand rupees per month—I was in limbo. I was a refugee waiting for my future to be decided by people to whom I had no access. I had no telephone, no address and no name. Immigration applicants were not allowed to go to the embassy without an invitation. Things that used to be small now became symbols of freedom and happiness to me: driving and owning a car, possessing a passport, reclining on my furniture, our sofas. The life I had had in the States so many years ago seemed like a fabrication told to me by someone else, not a life I myself had enjoyed, a life in which I had prospered.

At the end of our second year in New Delhi, we received a letter from the embassy: the invitation for an emigration interview. The day for which we had suffered together for two years had finally arrived. At the interview, the officer asked my father to name his children—all eleven of us. My father, who had been a governor most of his career, took the questions and the interview casually. He named his sons, but neglected to mention my brother who was sponsoring us. Perhaps he assumed it was implicit and that the officer knew this minor fact already. This lapse in communication delayed our case another year; we had to provide an affidavit to prove our sponsor really was our brother.

We got the visa. By then I was both physically and mentally damaged: tuberculosis had already lodged itself in my slight frame and was diagnosed in Canada only a year later; an entrenched depression has required me to rely on antidepressants until the present day. Nevertheless, together we flew to Canada to join my brother. My parents, my sister and I flew from India, and my two brothers from Pakistan. I didn't want anybody to know the date of my brothers' arrival from Pakistan—I thought it was too good to be true, to go smoothly without trouble. Their arrival at Toronto Pearson International Airport has remained an ecstatic memory in my mind.

Chapter XVI

Embracing Marginality

A lucky Afghan, I was able to flee my country's twenty-two years of fighting and uncertainty to find refuge in the peaceful, developed country of Canada. Day by day, as I recovered and became accustomed once more to comfort and convenience, I heard news of a dead-end struggle for survival in my home country. The country and the people were all so dear to me that I couldn't stop watching their stories on television.

I was in India when, in 1989, the Soviet soldiers withdrew from Afghanistan. It was in 1992, one year after I came to Canada, that the Communist regime of Dr. Najibulla was ousted by the coalition of *Mujahideen*. Joy was rampant among the Afghan population the world over: the freedom fighters had won and the Soviets had been defeated. But the joy was short lived. Not much changed in the civil strife that followed, except that Afghans fought each other instead of Russians and Communists.

Soon the seven indigenous groups divided again, each killing the others in an attempt to take control of Kabul, and in so doing they ruined the city. The villagers, those who had remained behind and had not fled across Afghanistan's borders, were once again trapped between warring factions and ruthless warlords. Soviet atheism was replaced by a distorted fundamentalism decreed by zealous foreign invaders with nationalistic local militias.

Officially and unofficially, women were the focus of the agenda. Officially, the government first imposed wearing the headscarf and then gradually discouraged women from school and work outside of the home. Unofficially, women were the target of wealthy warlords and their entourages of thugs. Rape, kidnapping and forced marriages became routine.

Many families with young girls fled the country then. Many parents married their teenage daughters to any Afghan who came from the West and showed a passport. In that way, the family rescued the life of their girl and invested in a precarious source of income for themselves. I know many stories about women who became victims of that period. Soraya's is one that has always stayed in my mind.

I met Soraya in 1997, in a small town in Ontario. She was my sister's friend's sister and had just arrived from Afghanistan. We heard she had settled nearby, and went to visit her one weekend. She appeared excited and grateful to be in Canada. She was living in a small apartment with another Afghan family and had a grocery store job that required little English. Her apartment was outfitted simply with random furniture and the basics. I asked her how she had managed to reach Canada, who sponsored her and the like. How she opened up amazed me beyond my expectation.

"My life story is very tragic," Soraya began. Before I could ask why, she released it all in one breath—one breath for her, but by the time we heard the whole story, the entire day was spent.

She told us:

> From 1992 to 1996, during the *Mujahideen* government in Afghanistan, women were still working in a few public organizations, such as radio and television stations. They had to wear modest Islamic clothes, but they were not forbidden to work. I was a successful television newscaster and had many fans among young people. They said I had a lovely voice and I hosted poetry programs late at night. I loved literature and wanted to pursue a career in the field. I was in my third year of university and was thinking about going abroad for higher education, but that seemed like a dream at the time.

Soraya was confirming what I had heard about the *Mujahideen's* government: the country was a floating shipwreck of divided tribal, religious and feudal power. The different groups of *Mujahideen* were locked in a constant struggle for control of the government. Hope for the future was a remote illusion, and stability a fantasy. Life itself seemed like a vague memory of a distant dream for the citizens. Death had its wings spread over the city. Dying was an easy escape from routine torture.

Young people were killed in numbers for no reason. Social gatherings of friends would end in violence and death over heated discussions on political views. Young soldiers and militants used their guns as toys and would fire on people over childish games or a package of hashish; guns were also often fired by mistake, killing soldiers and innocent people. Sometimes people were killed in order to terrorize an area. Women were trapped inside their homes. Young women and girls lived in constant fear of kidnapping, open attack or conspiracy.

The term "coffin puller" became known among families with young, unmarried girls. Coffin pullers—so-called because they "pulled" girls from their homes—were soldiers of a powerful warlord in the North, the top-ranking commander who routinely selected girls from the streets, their homes, and even from among wedding convoy guests and brides-to-be. A man would spot and track a desirable girl, and a few days later his thugs would kidnap her, taking her to one of the militia's many homes in a remote part of the city. Families had no recourse. Once a thug stole a girl, she belonged to his territory. Soraya had been a victim of that brutality.

We were very afraid. People told me I was beautiful and well known, I had better be careful. But I didn't know how I could take care. I had felt the threat once or twice when I received anonymous letters and compliments.

One grey evening in December, my life took a turn. I finished work at the TV station and stepped out to get some fresh air before the hired car would be ready to take me home. A big man with a black turban—a mark of the General's people—appeared right in front of me. Startled, I stepped back. My heart sank with fear as the man approached me. I saw revulsion in his big, round eyes. His protuberant nose shaded a considerable scar on his left cheek. He wore all-black Afghan clothing: a long shirt over ample trousers, a vest, and a shawl that hung loosely from his arms and wrapped around one side of his body. His air disgusted me. Reflexively, I moved away, but he blocked me. He cleared his throat, murmured that his commander had sent something for me and produced a small note from his vest pocket. I became numb and dizzy. I felt the whole building shifting behind me, like I was breaking into pieces. The man pushed the note into my hand and disappeared. I knew I was in very deep trouble. Once a commander chose a woman, he would have her no matter what it would take.

I collected my wits and walked to the driver, who was calling me from the station wagon that shuttled the newscasters to our homes. My parents would be waiting for me as usual. From the car, I had to walk about twenty metres to my front door. My mother worried continually about this distance and had warned me to be alert. I always told her not to worry, the area was well lit. But that night was different. I kept the note clutched in my hand during the drive home while pretending to be engaged in the conversation going on around me. I finally lodged the note in my pocket and tried to forget about its searing presence in my life, but I knew these notes usually contained orders to report to the commander's house or else be kidnapped by his people. The car service let me off and I said goodbye to my colleagues as usual. The next part, the twenty metres to my home, was the longest distance of my life. My heart was pounding. Finally, I reached the door and threw myself inside.

My family guessed what had happened. It was inevitable, though none of us could accept it. My mother wrung her hands, murmuring something that sounded like profanity; my sister stood motionless, as if moving would make it worse; my father paced and scratched his short grey hair, clearing his throat from time to time. I took a deep breath before I could speak. I knew it—I knew I would be the unlucky one of all the women and girls at the station. Before I could speak again, I burst into sobs. The whole family was grief-stricken.

I was stunned; it didn't sound real to me. I had heard about the coffin pullers and their ambushes, had written short fiction about them, but hearing a real story from a real person was stunning. Soraya, too, was telling the story as though she had read it somewhere. Was she connected to her past or was it a nightmare she was describing? I couldn't tell. My sister also surprised me with her cool indifference to Soraya's story. Later she told me that she had heard about it before from others. Soraya stopped to offer us more cake and sweets and to pour more tea, but I was anxious to hear the rest of her story.

"So, what did your parents do?" I asked.

She shook her head and said:

Oh my God! They were hysterical. My mother was wailing and pulling her hair, asking why must her intelligent, beautiful daughter face that horrible fate? My father choked back his own sobs and withdrew to another room while I read the note to my mother and sister. After hours of crying in agony and despair, my family was able to swallow the fact of our tragedy and begin thinking of a strategy for escape.

It was well past midnight when my father announced his decision: In the next several days, mother was to flee Kabul for Pakistan with my sister and me. My mother was torn, considering her home and the valuable things she had collected over so many years.

She agreed that we would leave, but wanted to take care of our belongings first. She also wanted to share the news with her parents. My grandmother was weak and fragile; my mother didn't want to give her a heart attack by disappearing without notice. But my father insisted and convinced her to depart the next evening with my sister and me, leaving all her lovely things behind with him. My sister and I were concerned for our father's safety: what would happen to him if the commander's men came and found me gone? We feared he would be put in prison or worse. My father assured us that he would find a way to escape if such a thing happened.

That was how many families escaped Afghanistan. In order to avoid suspicion by the government, families would pretend they were going to visit a friend. Early on, during the planning stages of such an exodus, families might discretely sell their belongings to various second-hand shops. But later, when fleeing became necessary, they could uproot readily and leave their skeletal homes intact. The fear of rumour and detection was so great, many families wouldn't even inform close relatives of their plans.

Escaping families worried about being arrested, robbed or injured along the way. They needed to broker an exodus through an individual with connections at both locations in order for an escape to take place in relative safety. A family would leave Kabul early in the morning with very little luggage; near the Pakistani border, they would abandon their car and walk hidden routes through rough terrain often riddled with landmines. After crossing into Pakistan, they would be picked up by an arranged car and driven to Peshawar.

I asked Soraya exactly how she and her family had left Kabul.

She smiled and said:

> I think my mother was still considering the fate of each and every piece of her home and all that filled it when we heard a disturbance outside. She jumped out of bed and started whispering what it could be to

my father. I thought I heard something, too.

My father tried to reassure us and told us it must have been the wind, but my mother started praying, asking God to keep our family from shame and grief.

Again, we heard footsteps—stealthy this time as they drew closer. Rationally, we knew what was happening, but in our hearts we could not accept it.

My mother grabbed the holy book from its shelf and covered it with ineffectual kisses, saying, "Oh holy book, save my daughters! You are the only refuge I have on my side. Save me and I'll vow that for nine months—" But before my mother finished her prayers, our door shook under heavy banging. My sister and I hid behind my mother. In seconds, three big men invaded our corridor and thrust themselves into the living room. I recognized the scarred messenger.

"What do you want from us?" demanded my father, poised as a gentleman before the thugs. "Tell us and leave!"

"Your daughter knows," the scarred man said sarcastically. 'There is no need to put on an act. The commander will have your daughter. Whether you behave well or not only makes a difference in what you get from him later.'

His entourage of thugs joined in and advised my parents not to worry. They said I would be happy with the commander, showered with jewels and money. I shook, clinging to my mother's back.

My father began pleading, his former composure evaporated in the face of our brutal reality. He was almost yelling that he couldn't give his daughter to the robber of people's honour. He went on to say that the commander was a rapist, unafraid of God; he was talking of Islam, but what kind of Islam was this? My father firmly said that he was not going to give his child to that robber! But he was muted by a blow to the back of his neck with a metal cable. I screamed. My father lay flat on the floor.

The thugs ordered me to get ready, but I clung frozen to my mother. "Don't come near my daughter or I'll kill you myself!" my mother shouted as the men disentangled me from her.

The trauma lasted only a moment or so and ended with me being dragged behind the men, my mouth stuffed with a shawl. My mother and sister ran up and down the stairs, banging on doors, begging neighbours to help us. The neighbours came out and stood beside my mother as I was dragged away.

I later learned that my mother stood at our doorstep every night after that, waiting for me to come home.

My sister no longer slept peacefully and my father never fully recovered from the injury to his head and his soul. My parents managed to arrange my sister's safe passage to Pakistan, where she lived with relatives. My mother refused to leave the country. She waited for me to return.

Soraya was upset now. Tears filled her eyes. I thought maybe her mother had died and she was remembering her. We all became silent.

Soraya gathered herself quickly. "More tea?" she asked.

I took my cup out for more green tea. I had hundreds of questions seeking a hundred more details of where they had taken her, but the words froze in my mouth. I had heard and read stories of young women disappearing to the notorious commander's harem. Relatives of victims were silent about their daughters' destinies: they either didn't know or chose not to. For them it wasn't just about losing a daughter, it was losing their honour in shame and weakness. I was dying to know more about the other side of the wall the commander had built, separating life from agony and horror.

Soraya apologized for getting carried away in her story and not attending to us. She got up to bring fruit. I asked my sister if it was okay to ask Soraya about what happened to her in the commander's house and she thought that it was. When I asked, Soraya didn't hesitate.

I was taken to a big house. Many young women were there, the commander's young wives, each one snatched from her home or from the street. I was taken to a room furnished with velvet pillows and mattresses.

A few hours after my arrival the first night, the commander appeared. He was short, fat and round-bellied, with a sarcastic smile. He wore a common long shirt and baggy trousers with a shawl hanging from his shoulders. Feigning a gentleman's manner, he ambled in with his feet apart. I had heard about his features and form, but it was completely jarring to behold him. With his bug-like eyes, he looked around him, pretending he was more interested in how I was being kept than in what or who I was.

In a voice that sounded more like a yell, he said my name. Avoiding my eyes, he looked around and asked if I was provided with everything I needed. I burst into tears and shrieked that I wanted freedom; I called him "coffin puller"; I berated him for what he had done to me, crying that I was a young girl with many dreams to work for. Before I had finished, he sat right next to me and acted as if I had come to ask his help. I shivered seeing his fat body rolling towards me.

He softly said that everything would be okay and I would be happy soon. Still avoiding my gaze, he murmured that he had arranged for my *nikah*. He said it with such pride, as if he had done me a huge favour, implying that the *nikah* and reciting a few verses from the holy Quran would end my parents' agony and calm the storm in all of our minds.

I didn't know what to say. I wanted to vomit. Shattering all my dreams and kidnapping me from my sheltered life with my parents was, to him, all resolved by a *Mullah* reading a statement. My life was ruined. The fact that many other young girls in his house shared my fate only increased my pain. We were all helpless, imprisoned by his lust.

The commander arranged for an awkwardly choreographed ritual with a man who recited the Quran and held forth about our being according to Islam; the commander wanted to pretend his forced marriage with me was an Islamic act. Like puppets, all present pretended that this five minutes recitation from the holy book resolved my vehement disagreement and restored balance, ensuring my nuptial fidelity.

It was an awkward scene for me. I had no say in it. In Islamic *nikah*, the acceptance of the wife is required, but there the *Mullah* didn't even ask me if I accepted the marriage.

"So, Soraya, how did you come here?" The question popped out of my mouth.

Soraya burst into laughter, proud and free.

For me, the fight began there. From the moment I was dragged to that house, I began plotting my escape. I learned later that my mother shared my mission; she had begun the night I was abducted. She met with everyone who could influence the commander. She also met with others who might help rescue me. Within the commander's house, I talked to the servants, gave them money, asked them to take my messages home. I didn't know exactly where I was. From the journey's duration, I knew I was not in Kabul.

One of the commander's servants, a reasonable man, seemed to be looking out for me. On a hunch, I took a chance and gave him some of the money, gold and jewelry which the commander showered upon me with each visit to my chamber. In return, the manservant sought ways to obtain news about my mother. I implored him to mail out my letters to my mother instructing her to locate someone to help me escape. After a week he had received assurance that my letters had gotten to my mother.

In the coming days, I pretended to relinquish my reluctant stance towards the commander. It was only one night a week that I was forced to accommodate his visits to my room. Otherwise, I was left to myself. He brought me gold necklaces and rings on those nights, presuming that for the rest of the week I would be amused. But I just bequeathed the trinkets and baubles to the kindly manservant.

Highly agitated, the servant came one day with news from my mother. The pitiful man was rightfully frightened of reprisals: if our complicity were discovered he would be tortured and killed and his family would suffer extreme hardship. His salary from the commander fed his extended clan. I gave him a big gold ring and asked him not to worry.

My mother's message indicated that I should wait until she managed to get help from an international agency. He didn't know whether it was the UN, the Human Rights Commission or an international women's organization—all he knew was that it was an international agency.

Too much time passed. One evening, the man arrived and warily told me to get ready. He said I would be fetched in an hour.

Where? How? By whom? I didn't know, but I knew my mother had found a way.

The servant was shaking with fear and haste. He ordered me to get dressed, to leave everything behind and wait at the corner of the house where nobody would notice me. He was in such a bad mood I dared not speak. I donned my scarf and shoes and strolled to the far corner of the house. It was the first time in months that I thought of the other women in the house as people. I could perhaps have come to like them and imagined the house as just a place in which to live. It was the first time I felt like a human being among other human beings; my sense that I existed in this world was renewed. I was being rescued, although I had no idea how. It was March 25, just five days after *Nawroz*, our new year.

It was evening, a quarter to six, when I heard a motor overhead. A helicopter circled the commander's compound. I wondered what was going on. I had heard the commander had helicopters, but wasn't certain. The whop-whopping of the helicopter blades drew closer. I watched the helicopter descending, growing bigger until it landed in the courtyard beside the house.

My manservant rushed at me and whispered, "Go!"

I felt ecstatic, transported to another dimension. I rushed toward the huge piece of green metal roaring before me, propellers billowing dust. I thought I saw a woman waving at me from the window. I felt like I was flying, in a dream, on clouds. The manservant shoved me inside the helicopter then I felt a woman's arms around me. I heard a woman's cry. It was my mother.

Soraya burst into laughter and sobs. Tears were rolling down her cheek. Giggles mixed with cries. I cried, too. We all did: Soraya, my sister and I.

"Good for your mother," I said.

> Yes. Indeed! My mother had asked a Canadian women's centre for help and they had managed the rest. I was home, but I was no longer a young unmarried girl who would receive proposals. I was a woman, a wife, a victim of the commander. My future was ruined. My reputation scarred beyond repair...

Soraya paused here. She couldn't go further. She had to pause from the painful memory. She then said how the international Canadian agency helped her become a refugee in Canada.

Soraya, like all Afghan and Muslim girls whose virginity has been forcibly taken, felt she had been robbed of her social and human identity and could therefore never deserve a husband. But she was happy, she said, proud of her job at the grocery store, proud to have escaped the commander and relieved to be away from the community which now viewed her as his victim.

I had heard that many stories like Soraya's happened to young, beautiful girls, but had never before felt it was so real and so close. When we left Soraya's house, I told my sister how brave she was to share so intimate a story with us.

"Everyone has heard about it," said my sister, smirking. "Soraya has changed, she used to be very beautiful and famous."

As we drove home from Soraya's house, I thought of the many

other girls whose mothers had not been able to rescue them: girls kidnapped on their way to school; brides snatched from wedding-decorated cars and ferreted straight to the commander's house; and too many more unaccounted for, each deserving to have her life's story fully recorded. It hurt even more once we knew that the same commander was one of the powerful figures in the new Afghan government, continuing to get away with crimes.

Sometime later I heard Soraya had sponsored an older widower, a demanding, cantankerous man. When I asked why she chose him, my sister said, "Well, no young single man would marry someone who has been kidnapped by the commander." I had nothing to say to her.

Soraya's abysmal story was typical of Afghan women. I met many more whose lives were destroyed or who related second-hand accounts of others whose had been ruined. By the sheer fact of their existence, Afghan women became the central focus for any government that took power in Afghanistan. The Communists killed husbands and sons while giving women work under the guise of liberation. The *Mujahideen* forced women from the public sector in the name of Islam, enclosing them within their private homes with weapons and money.

In 1996, the Taliban government legitimized terror and discrimination against women, again in the name of Islam and protection: they swept women from society altogether, deftly robbing them of their citizenship, their identity and their right to public space. Using law revision, whips and stoning, the Taliban ordered women to become invisible, silent and idle.

Legislation included rescinding access to education, to work, to equal rights and to existing outdoors, as a woman might be a temptation to hapless men who, God help them, were only men and therefore could not be expected to restrain their natural urges. Wearing white shoes, high heels, showing a finger while buying bread, having a slightly larger grill in one's burqa to see a little more or reaching for air while enduring an asthma attack—all were crimes that made Taliban guards beat the hell out of women with sticks and whips.

Some insist there were no rapes during the Taliban's reign, no kidnapping of brides and young girls from the street. Instead, I think the Taliban employed alternative forms of terror and oppression: they revoked women's right to public and outdoor life.

Chapter XVII

Stoning Innocence

Jamal was one of our family friends who immigrated to Canada after suffering under Taliban rule in Kabul. During the civil wars and *Mujahideen* she had remained in Kabul, but could not bear to live under Taliban rule. She escaped to Pakistan and from there got sponsored to come to Toronto. While she related many personal experiences with the Taliban, there is one account that is carved into my brain. It is the story of a woman stoned to death, which Jamal herself witnessed.

I had seen a video of the Taliban shooting a woman in a burqa in the national stadium on television, but it had never sunk in as real. When Jamal told me that she had seen the stoning of a woman with her own eyes, at first I didn't believe her. When she insisted, I became eager to hear it exactly the way she had seen it.

"Where were you when that happened? How come you were present at the scene? When was it?" I bombarded Jamal with questions, one after another.

Jamal started to tell me how the men threw stones at the woman. I asked her to tell me from the very beginning how she had managed to witness the stoning. She had probably told the story many times; as she opened her mouth the words followed smoothly. She said, "All right. I will tell you exactly how I saw it. Do you have the patience for it? Do you really want to hear it? Many women don't want to."

"Oh, I do. I do. Tell me everything," I said, and became all ears as Jamal told the story.

I was living in Jalalabad at that time. That day, I was going to Kabul. The buses were leaving that morning so they could reach Kabul by sunset. I wanted to postpone the trip for a day, but who knew if the roads would be open the next day? Who knew if travelling would be safe at all? I had to leave that day to reach my sick mother.

I took my eleven-year-old nephew with me as my *Mahram*, since I was not allowed to travel alone. He was considered a "man" who might accompany me. We finally reached the bus station and boarded a bus going to Kabul. The bus slowly filled with weary travellers. It was early afternoon when the seats were finally filled with girls and young women accompanied by elderly and bearded men—young men without a long beard were scared of being arrested and avoided travelling as much as they could.

The bus driver alighted finally, spat out the window, murmured a brief prayer and gunned the engine, which groaned over the unpaved roads to Kabul. The city disappeared behind us in minutes and our trip took us along the old mountain roads.

Remembering the twisted, narrow roads and the high mountains of the Kabul–Jalalabad highway that I had taken most of the winter weekends many years ago, I asked Jamal, "Are the roads still dangerous and narrow?"

Jamal started laughing at my naïveté. "What you saw then were dream roads for us now. Remember it used to take you guys two hours to get from Kabul to Jalalabad? It used to take us seven hours at least, assuming there were no incidents on the way. Forget about that glorious past of yours, try to imagine what I tell you about now," Jamal said.

"Okay. Continue. What happened then?"

We had not been underway more than an hour before the bus stopped unexpectedly. I woke from a light doze to the prayers of the people around me. I knew something was happening. I thought there were robbers who would tie up the bus driver and kick him unconscious, then rob the passengers of their belongings. But out the window I saw our bus driver relaxing over a snuff of *naswar* that he removed from his pocket and brought up to his nose. Other bus drivers joined him; it seemed that our bus was not the only one stopped. The male passengers got off the buses, women remained within. A woman who was sitting near the door asked the driver what was happening.

"Nothing," he told her. "Stay in the bus."

One of the elderly men climbed back into the bus. We, the women, questioned him, but he told us it was none of our business. It was clear from the buzz that something was seriously wrong. Death and fear were in the air. The faces of the men were downcast.

A young boy accompanying his mother re-boarded the bus, shouting, "The judge is here! The district governor is here! There is a court!"

Questions were fired at the boy, so he promised to survey the scene for us and jumped out of the bus, pretending he belonged with the men. Apparently, we were stopped at a square that was used to hold local courts.

I couldn't take it any longer. I tied my *chadari* around me and got off the bus, ignoring the hysterical murmur of the women. Reaching the crowd, I stood behind a thin line of men encircling the makeshift court arena.

It sounded like stories I had read in the newspapers and magazines in the West. When the Taliban were in control of the government in Afghanistan, many Westerners who visited Afghanistan—or even Pakistan—wrote about how women were treated by them. No matter how much I had read or heard about it, it always remained a clouded picture to me. As Jamal was talking and I was trying to imagine the scene, the facts were getting confused with the horror of my imagination.

"I can't believe this, Jamal! How did you travel those days? You didn't get scared to be around all those men alone?" I interrupted. Jamal was not taking me seriously by then; she knew I couldn't take all that intensity and terror.

"Listen! What have you heard? Let me tell you what I saw there, what was going on." She continued:

> A large bag in the centre of the crowd was tied with a knot around its top. Like a living creature, the bag was moving.

> *"Allah Akbar!"* cried a tall, burly man with a dark beard and long black hair, gesturing for the men to come forward. His was an invitation to throw stones at the moving bag. As each stone pelted the bag, a shriek and moan arose from it: the sound of dying.

> I was in a panic and asked the men around me what was happening. I asked an elderly man standing in front of me. He got mad and yelled, "Are you blind? Don't you see there is a stoning order? They're stoning Nawab's daughter to death."

> "Islamic brothers!" again came the call from the huge man in black. "Adultery is forbidden in Islam

and here is the adulterer condemned to death by stoning. Throw your stones at the miserable *siyasar*! She has been deceived by the devil, beat her!" He continued bellowing, neglecting to mention that two persons are required to commit adultery and only one—the woman—was being punished here. "Allah is Great!" he screamed.

Extolling the wonders of God, he threw a sharp stone squarely at the bag. The bag was still moving, resembling hunted quarry, perhaps an injured bird trying to flap its wings, heaving itself from one spot to another. Dark blood seeped from the bag and was absorbed by the dry soil. Then, there was a renewed cry from the men for another round of stoning, as the adulterer was obviously not yet dead. The bag looked like a red, flowered shawl wrapped around a lifeless thing. The rabble continued their fervent cries and stoning.

I was overcome with the morbid desire to get closer to the bag so I could hear the voice of the woman dying inside the flowered shawl. Suddenly, a turbaned old man pushed to the front of the crowd to stand beside the bag.

"This is my daughter," he cried loudly. "She has no sin. Don't do this, for God's sake! Don't kill her!" In despair, the old man unwrapped his turban and threw it into the pooling blood at the base of the bag.

"Your honour, Judge!" sobbed the old man over the bag. "Sir, Governor! Oh, brothers, why should you stone an innocent human being before knowing the truth? This is a sin. This woman belongs to me. She is my daughter. She is not guilty of anything. This man, this non-Muslim here who has sued my daughter, who has blamed her for adultery, he is lying. He is the guilty one, not my daughter. My daughter was not yet born when she was engaged to this man. When my girl was born, this lad left the country. Disappeared! My daughter waited twenty years for him, in accordance with the law. When he still did not return, she married another man and has been married for ten years. She is a mother with three young children. Her husband was killed in the war. She is supporting her family. Who is this man to accuse her of adultery? He is not her husband! Where was he these thirty years that now he shows up with these accusations? Oh, my girl, they have killed you for nothing! You are a martyr!"

"Do not cry, brother. It's okay," the judge called out. "It must have been a misunderstanding. Brothers! Nawab's daughter is a martyr. She will go to heaven and be forgiven by God."

The flowered bag containing the martyr flopped to its side. As the crowd dispersed slowly, the elderly rubbed their palms together, perhaps pondering thoughts of their own death. Others, probably confused and bewildered, thought perhaps about their strength, their superiority over women, the dark-headed sinners, torture and crime.

Perhaps the old man recalled his daughter's childhood. Soon all that there remained in the judicial arena was him; the bloody, flowered bag; and the spread of sunset.

"Sister! Are you coming or not?" The angry call of our driver startled me. I rushed toward the bus and boarded. "Sister had a vantage point to see everything!" said the driver sarcastically, producing a few fake coughs and starting the bus as I took my seat quietly. A martyr had been born. I had witnessed it.

Jamal's story ended there. I felt lost. I couldn't figure out how anyone could justify such killing. Endless questions consumed my mind about justice, men, the Taliban, right and wrong. Now, every time I hear or read about a woman being stoned to death, I feel like I was there when Nawab's daughter became a martyr.

Chapter XVIII

Defying the Cover

When I heard stories of women's hardship under the Taliban regime and how they were stripped of their civil rights, I thought of those women I met under the Communist regime in Kabul, those who were forced to become the breadwinners of their family and, ironically, gained a kind of self-empowerment in the role. Those were the women who had lost their husbands and sons during the Communist era and were given jobs in factories and fields. Some of these women felt a sense of accomplishment and success in working, which was the only compensation for the misery and torture their families had endured.

I thought of a young woman I met years ago in a factory. She looked pale and weak. Her husband had been killed in the war, her house demolished by a rocket.

"I lost everything, my husband, my house, but I was able to rescue my children," she said. "I am making enough money to pay for their school, as well as their food and clothing."

"Are you happy to work or not?" I asked.

"Of course! I can even buy myself jewellery once in a while," she confessed, glancing at the gold ring on her finger.

"Would you give up your job if you were able to get support from somewhere else?" I asked.

"Who would support me?" she answered, confounded. "No. It feels good to take care of yourself and your children. What would I do at home anyway? Haven't I worried enough?"

By choice or by force, she and other women gained confidence and independence; how would they react to yet another prescribed position? The Communists forced women to work, and the *Mujahideen* pushed women back into being passive citizens. During that period women became imprisoned by their gender and sexuality, and the Taliban robbed them of their social identity and basic freedom. The Taliban charged women for being female—their faces, their nails, their hair, their voices and their footsteps became targets of terror and violence enforced by the government.

But there was one area in which women did work during the Taliban government: healthcare. The Taliban logic of no-working-women failed them in medicine; they couldn't do without women doctors because, by their laws, no woman patient could be seen by a male doctor, so female doctors had to be allowed to work. One women's hospital existed for the entire country, but female doctors were able to work within the main city hospitals' health system, as it served both men and women.

My cousin was a gynecologist working in a hospital in Charikar, the capital of Parwan province, located one hundred kilometres north of Kabul. Separately, she ran a clinic out of her home that was always crowded with female patients from remote villages. She said her professional and financial life was never more fulfilled than during those days. She saved many women's lives, made many families happy and saved many children, too. "It was at the hospital," she said, "that the orders and restrictions were degrading."

I sponsored her to come to Toronto with her husband and son. Many nights at her house I listened to her stories from the *Mujahideen* and Taliban eras: stories of women who had been raped by their relatives, forced to abort their children because of poverty, kept away from a doctor until they were dying; stories of being insulted, beaten and terrorized by Taliban guards.

Her account of a typical day at the hospital made me think deeply.

> I was allowed to work at the hospital on the condition that I wear a burqa and work only with female patients. Male doctors were not allowed to treat female patients. Although my house was near the hospital, it was difficult to walk wearing the *chadari*. The first couple of times I wore it, I tripped all the way to the hospital. I asked the Taliban for permission to go to work without the *chadari* because I had a problem with my left leg that made it even more difficult to walk. They agreed, but told me to wear a large shawl that would cover my entire body.
>
> In the hospital, some other female coworkers and I

worked completely segregated from the men; we had our own operating room on one side of the hospital. We rarely saw our male colleagues and when we did there was no communication. The days in the hospital were very busy and exhausting. We had many critical patients: women with complications from childbirth, suffering complicated labour, and many others injured by rockets, bombs and land mines. All were severe cases and all demanded prompt attention. Many of our patients died soon after their arrival. Many couldn't make it through surgery. Many lost their babies. Women were usually brought to us too late. Their husbands wouldn't bring them to the hospital until every other option had been exhausted.

One evening when I was on duty, I heard the cries of a woman and rushing footsteps in the lobby. It was the usual: a dying woman carried into the emergency room by her hysterical family. The young woman had been wounded by rockets. She was unconscious and bleeding profusely, her face pale and dry, a blood-soaked blanket draped over her. An old woman, her mother, had carried her on her back from a village almost twenty miles away.

"For God's sake save my daughter's life!" she wailed. "She is pregnant and her husband is not here. He is in Pakistan. How will I be able to face her husband? Oh, my little baby daughter!"

Removing the blanket to examine her wounds, I determined the operation would be impossible for me to perform alone. One other doctor was on duty, a male. I shouted to the nurse to go and get Ahmed, the male doctor. She hesitated. She was afraid. I shouted at her to go and get him.

Ahmed raced to the operating room. We said nothing of the crime we were about to commit. We cared only that a human life was in our hands. According to the Hippocratic Oath we swore upon graduation from medical school, a patient's life is a doctor's first priority. Ahmed and I were progressing well with the procedure when the operating door slammed open. A Taliban guard barged in, a big shawl and Kalashnikov rifle slung around his shoulder. My sleeves were rolled up and my scarf lay on a chair. I knew it was wrong in the Taliban's eyes, but I continued my work. Ahmed also kept his focus. A shadow rose in my peripheral vision and came down on Ahmed. With his baton, the guard had struck Ahmed's back.

"Aren't you ashamed of yourself to operate on a woman? You sinner!" yelled the guard. "Shameless bastard!"

Anger and grief from Ahmed's glance spoke volumes, although he said nothing as the guard dragged him by his gown out the door, yelling, "You, doctor, cover your hands and head! Why are you women so shameless?" The guard addressed me without looking at me.

Consumed with disgust as I was, I blocked out what I did at the time. Later, my nurses told me I had yelled at the guard to get lost. Luckily, my patient recovered, but Ahmed was punished: fired and fined two months' salary. The surprisingly lenient warning I received stated that if in future I didn't abide by the Taliban laws, I, too, would be punished. I didn't wait to be punished; I already had been punished in so many ways. I escaped to Pakistan.

In Toronto, my cousin the doctor has no job and no way to use her training to help make a difference in people's lives. But she is free. Free in the limited way of one who is bound by memory. The Taliban still haunt her sleep.

Chapter XIX

Exile

I am a Canadian citizen, happy and free. But life in exile is not like a first-choice settlement. It is a settlement just over the edge; it is like balancing on a curb. Life carries on like a slow boat that bumps into every little rock in the shallows. Life doesn't move forward or it moves so fast that you lose track of where you are.

Thirty years ago, when I was a student in the United States, I represented an exotic country and had the luxury of feeling unique. With the Russian invasion of Afghanistan, I became a first-hand resource. With the *Mujahideen* in power, I was sought after as one who had insight into women's lives under such a regime. While the Taliban hosted Bin Laden in Afghanistan, I was an expert on women in Islam.

We are stuck in the mud, I think. Our feet are heavy, our souls are heavy, even our ears are stopped up. I listened one day to our local Canadian radio newscaster passing shallow judgments about immigrants and refugees: "Immigrants come here to be wealthy," he proclaimed.

Wealth? What wealth? I wondered. Is wealth really the number of dollars you accumulate in your bank account or is it the number of days you feel on top of the world, living fully? What about the days when you feel like a lonely piece of shit in a foreign place? Or the years you suffered prior to your arrival in a free land?

When I was a child, everybody around me—my parents, teachers, aunts and uncles—all promised a future replete with success, happiness and satisfaction. Most of all, the future was composed of freedom. They promised that the only price we had to pay to reach that future was to work very hard and discipline ourselves. It seemed to me that they were telling us not to have any fun, because we would have all the fun we wanted once we reached the future.

Being the kind of kid who believed adults, I invested all my time and effort in my education. I never allowed myself any free time at university because I engaged in every opportunity to study or earn money to reach that future. Since graduate education wasn't available in my country, I was saving to go abroad to further my education. While my friends had fine clothes and makeup, I was prepared for the future. It is the future that never arrives. I felt only a breeze that smelled faintly of future. There was nothing to grasp, no moment to seize.

We immigrants planned our futures intending to remain and invest in our own country. We had not planned to lose track of our lives midway. We left our county in order to survive; to become wealthy was beside the point. The point was to live. We have a life, but it is peripheral. I only see the irony of it now, much later, as a highly educated woman, no longer the shy, dark girl of my puberty. I have been—women of Afghanistan have been—second-rate citizens twice: first as females, then again as immigrants. Or, perhaps, it is the same. To be a woman in my home country, my native land, is like being an immigrant from somewhere else.

It wasn't until I was a visible minority in a foreign country that I realized the layers and layers of separation that not only distinguished me from the mainstream population, but also existed within me, dividing memories of my childhood from my country's historic past. I came to my new country prepared to be a minority; I even visualized occasions upon which my accent, the colour of my eyes, hair and skin would set me apart. I was prepared for the awkward moments, perhaps a hard time relating to my new culture, and knew that my new culture might have a hard time relating to me.

I often felt irrelevant to the flow of time. Sometimes the flow of time was irrelevant to me. I became nostalgic for a time when I was central to my culture. But then, I realize that this is not a true nostalgia, it is merely a wish. My life as a woman under Taliban rule had neither been affected by the flow of time, nor had it been like a pebble thrown into water, rippling the waves of time around it. Is it possible that I can be this disingenuous with myself?

I never conceived of the possibility of living in the margins of society, but over time I have become accustomed to it. You are either native to a culture and a land or you are not. What culture was my body? What land was native to me? The marginality I experienced did not come from outside; it was within me. I lived an explicit marginality and an implicit marginality, the result is a fractured identity. Perhaps I overuse the term. Somewhere, in the small corner of memory where I see myself running through the courtyard wishing to keep clear of the dirty cook, I think there may not actually be a marginalized life—or a margin at all. How can there be a margin when there is no centre?

My first attempts to participate in Canadian society included training to become a cultural interpreter for non-English-speaking immigrant women who were victims of abuse and violence; I was certainly familiar with the issues of violence that women face. In this job, I learned not only how to conceptualize sexual abuse and violence, but also how to open this dialogue within myself. In my native languages, Dari and Pashto, there is no word for incest or sexual abuse. We have a term for "misuse"—*so e estefada*—which we use for the improper use of something. There is also a term for troubling and disturbing—*aazaar wa azyat*. At present, after the fall of the Taliban and with the involvement of international agencies for the advancement of women in Afghanistan, this term is used to mean abuse with regard to women. The word for violence—*khoshunat*—is also now being used to refer to violence against women.

When I learned the term "sexual abuse," I was astounded by its magnitude and oddly freed by the dimension it opened in my understanding. Rape is the only form of sexual abuse I'd been able to conceptualize in my own language, but still its definition is limited: rape of a woman by a stranger is the only form of "sexual abuse" that my native society acknowledges. Rape by strangers doesn't happen often in my native culture because women are not often seen in public. Yet rape is not an unusual crime at all, it is usually perpetrated against girls and women inside their homes, by relatives or servants. These silent crimes are not discussed.

The concept of rape inside the home by one's husband is beyond logic for men of my country—it is an accepted form of marital relation. I was shocked to learn the Western idea that a husband could be accused of raping a wife. Ingrained in me was the idea that husbands own their wives' bodies as property, the husband may do as he likes. Many women from my part of the world simply cannot conceive of the idea of rape between a husband and a wife.

I have found that if an action does not have a word to own it, its existence is denied. Naming something makes it real. Incrementally, I connected the unvoiced words to the volumes of literature on sexual violence; in this way, I was able to drag these new concepts up through the depths of my childhood. In the process, the concepts were visualized as my memories and my theories became the living experiences of thousands of women and girls who had tried to voice their pain over the years.

Ironically, life in exile—marginality—has enabled me to become whole. The separate parts and phases of my life that had been scattered in my native land came together in a foreign land. I finally located my deserted inner child. It was the five-year-old girl who was molested by the cook, Hasan. That girl was dark, so she was called ugly. She was unhappy, so she was called moody. She was frozen, so she was called cold. There was a world of distance between that dark child and me, as I was, I suppose, an immigrant from my childhood.

Occasionally, people ask about my past. Sometimes I answer, sometimes I don't. It sounds shallow, the past that cannot be connected to the present. For outsiders, it must seem thin and unreal. Even for some immigrants themselves, their past seems unreal. My brother, who was a successful television news editor in Afghanistan, began to doubt the accomplishments of his own past; in our new country, he drove a taxi. When people asked him about his past, he would tell them in his broken English. He began to wonder how they could possibly believe him when he could hardly believe it himself; the discrepancy was so great—a news editor and a taxi driver couldn't possibly be the same person. And, in a way, they weren't.

I, however, am searching for a deeper settlement, not so much in this society, but within me. I want to affirm all the layers of marginality in my life.

Chapter XX

The Governor

My father died in Canada with the same love for life and humanity that he'd always had. He was the most influential person in my life; I loved him more than anybody and anything. In childhood, he was my mirror of strength, wisdom, authority and beauty. I needed to believe he was making a genuine effort to evolve and be humane within the confines of his prescribed gender role. I acknowledge that, to this day, I confuse his authority with decency. He was handsome, tall, decisive and clear, and as a man in my culture he had all the necessary tools at his disposal to be so. In my youth, he appeared to become an understanding, supportive and open-minded father. In my adult life, he seemed an open book of moving life experience.

My father was an example of how much a human mind is capable of change. In fact, his life had evolved around contrasts: he grew from a poor religious student—a *Talib* in a *madrassa*—to a strict knowledgeable *Mullah*; then to an open-minded intellectual; later to an authoritative politician; and finally to an old man ready to embrace new ways of living as an immigrant in Toronto. He strove to love and question every layer of his life. His memories of childhood were of poverty. Stories of his own poverty interpreted poverty to me and connected me to the poor. He said that in childhood, he always wished to experience how it would feel to be full.

Later in life, when my father became a governor who lived comfortably and accepted modern ways of living for his children, he reflected on the contrasts upon which his life had evolved. He told us stories of his own father who was a strict religious leader and had opposed the very practices we enjoy today. He said that when my grandfather followed the sound of music in the village, the musicians would run away and my grandfather would go after them and break their instruments. Yet, my father not only liked music, but also encouraged us to learn to play and bought instruments for us.

My father himself had very strict codes of thinking and living. At age six he began studying as a *Talib*, which at the time was only a name for those who studied with a *Mullah*, and learned religious books, theological analysis and logic. Although his own father was a well-known scholar sought by *Talibs* who travelled to become his students, my father wanted to, like them, seek knowledge outside of the familiar range. To travel away from home was a way to devote one's life to learning. *Talibs* stayed with the *Mullahs* who became their teachers in the mosque. Like students everywhere, *Talibs* were the poorest people. They ate whatever the people brought for the *Mullah* in the mosque and sometimes went to houses asking for food. *Talibs* usually went home to visit at intervals after completing a portion of their studies.

My father related interesting stories about his life as a *Talib*, about how poor they were, how people respected them, and how their life was confined to books in the mosque and a life of poverty. He said they couldn't afford to light kerosene lamps for long hours, so he often studied by moonlight. Stories of my father as a *Talib* were a treat for us children to hear; some of his recollections convinced me that emotions and love find their way through poverty, isolation, restriction and distance.

My father insisted on girls' education and opened a school wherever we moved. He explained to us children that modern schooling was seen as taboo in his time, and he himself had been one of the kids who hid away from his village when government authorities sent for school registration. My father was unique in many ways, some acceptable to the norms of his people, some repulsive. But to me he was a person who was full of life, wit and dignity, a person with respect for himself and for others—though less for his wife, my mother. He died after a long struggle.

After his death, it became clear how much my father had shared his life and thoughts with us. As I was dreading losing him, his words comforted me and affirmed my feelings in every moment while dealing with the impending loss. I remember his remarks about what we children would be likely to feel when we lost him, about how to deal with sorrow, how it would surely subside with time, and how we should be realistic and accept it. Having a deep and thorough understanding of Islam, my father studied philosophy, sociology, and became a thinker with his own theories about life and creation. He also encouraged us, his children, to think, question, and reach a position of logic and knowledge. This logic made him a powerful governor, a good father and a strong person.

Whether or not it made him a good husband was probably beyond him. In fact, I think it simply didn't matter.

Chapter XXI

The Governor's Wife—My Mother

The short, chubby woman I had known as my weak-willed mother became even weaker in exile. After so many years of struggling to establish herself as a woman, a wife and a mother in our home country, she was completely sidelined by life in the new one. She did not speak the language; she didn't understand the culture or the lifestyle; she didn't belong here. But she struggled to fit, to be relevant and make it relevant for herself.

My mother became silent in her old age. She couldn't understand anything that was said to her in this new language and she could say nothing in return. She was even mute with her grandchildren—they didn't speak her language either—but she used her love and care to reach them. She used gestures to communicate, though she was often misinterpreted. It was as if even her body language didn't translate in a meaningful way.

She was my mother and she cared to know my friends, my co-workers and the people I dealt with every day. She would try to use the telephone, to no avail. She would often interpret messages by trying to read the tone and feeling in the voice on the other end;

sometimes, I actually thought it worked. My mother tried to get all the messages from her surroundings in this way, but it eventually failed her, time failed her, age failed her. She was halfway through the English alphabet when she became ill. She seldom complained, but managed to convince us to take her to the doctor at once.

We didn't believe she was sick; we interpreted her declining health within the stereotypes of old women back home. In my home country and within my own family, elderly women are easily neglected as they lack the strength to run the household, do chores and control a daughter-in-law's decisions. Elderly women often feign illness to attract attention; they are sometimes made to believe, as are elderly men, that sickness suits them better than health. When my mother finally complained of pain, we thought it was fake, just a symptom of her age and need for attention. She was weak and couldn't do chores, she lacked appetite. We thought we were stuck with a grumpy old lady.

And so, again, a woman became a victim. How could a woman who had never been allowed to assert herself in any way, who had spent a lifetime being silenced, fight off the ambush of disease? In her mind, she was old enough that she deserved to die: past the age of sixty while the usual life expectancy in Afghanistan is forty-three. She could not assert herself as a woman, she could not assert herself as an immigrant and now she could not assert herself on behalf of her own health.

My mother lay sick in the hospital. The whole experience was a mystery to her; she couldn't understand anything that was said to her, though she was trying to be an unimposing and polite patient.

She was obviously numb and hardly reacted to the poking and prodding. She knew she was sick. Her body was wasting away. The doctors couldn't find a diagnosis. We made decisions for her. She tried to wait patiently for the good news that would help her body heal.

I sat at the foot of my mother's hospital bed and, for the first time in my life, I felt something deep for that sick, tiny woman. She was in so much pain and so weak, yet she thought it was important to ask me where I went that day and what I'd done. It took so much out of her to ask me. She had become so small. This woman, who had nursed me and held me so that I might survive, was leaving. I let the past go. Or, the time vanished. I felt the comfort of sucking life from her breast. I had a new bond.

My mother died in the intensive care unit. "Thank you!" were the last words she spoke and the only words she knew in English, the only bridge to the doctors and the society in which she lived the last years of her life. How ironic that the words were an expression of gratitude; she was the perfect, unimposing guest to the end.

As I write this, I am shocked at how similar my mother and I are: she had no voice, no identity, yet she survived a marriage, had a family, ran a household, suffered hardship, grew and changed, and escaped the hell that my country became. I have a sense of identity and voice, which engenders this story. And that is all.

Glossary

Aday—Pashto
Pashto word meaning "mother."

"Allah Akbar"—Arabic
Phrase meaning " God is Great," used as a salutation.

Azan—Arabic
Call for prayers performed by mosque authorities (*Mullah* or his students) five times a day.

Chadari—Farsi/Dari
Word derived from *chadar*, which means scarf.
Whole body covering form of veil used only by Afghan women.

Fateha—Arabic
Islamic memorial service after the funeral held separately by the male and female members of the deceased's family.

Hajj—Arabic
Word for the pilgrimage to Mecca, one of the five pillars of Islam.

Jihad—Arabic
Holy war against offenders of Islam.

Khalq—Arabic
People

Khan—Farsi/Dari word used in both Farsi and Pashto
An influential, rich man in the community who usually holds a position of leadership.

Madrassa—Arabic
Islamic schools with strict rules where most Taliban have been trained in Pakistan.

Mahram—Arabic
Blood related member of the family such as siblings, spouse, parents and uncles/aunts.
Islam requires women to be accompanied in public by a male who is *Mahram* to them (husband, father, brother, uncle, son).

Muezzin—Arabic
A person who calls for prayers.

Mujahideen—Arabic
Holy warriors; those who fight in defence of Islam.
In the context of Afghanistan, it refers to those who resisted Soviet Invasion.
Singular form is *Mujahid.*

Mullah— Farsi word also used in Pashto
Religeous leader who leads prayers in the mosque.

Naswar—Farsi/Dari
A special kind of tobacco that people put under their tongues then spit out.

Nikah—Arabic
Islamic marriage vow usually performed for couples by the Islamic priest, *Mullah*.

Parcham—Farsi/Dari
Flag

Pashtun— Pashto
Ethnic group of people known to be the majority in Afghanistan, also living in Pakistan mainly in Federally Administered Tribal Area, Khyber-Pakhtunkhwa and Baloshistan.
Pashto is their language.

Qala—Arabic word used in both Pashto and Farsi/Dari
Big residences containing different quarters surrounded by tall walls and towers, similar to a fort.

Sadaqa—Arabic
Alms; a portion of earning that Muslims are required to give as alms to the poor.

Salam—used in Arabic, Farsi/Dari, Pashto in Afghanistan and by all Muslims
Greeting literally meaning "peace."
Short form of *Asalam-u-alaikum,* meaning "peace be upon you."

Sharia—Arabic
Islamic law and doctrine based on the Quran.

Shola—Arabic word also used in Dari
Flame

Siyasar—Farsi/Dari
Black-headed, a term widely used for women in public.

Talib—Arabic
Singular form of Taliban, meaning "seeker"; used for students of Islamic studies.

Toda—Farsi/Dari
People

Acknowledgments

Publishing a first book is always a tough fight. One has to be an established published author to penetrate publishing houses, but to be established is to have a publication. I twisted and turned in this crisscross path with my memoir for many years.

If Himani Bannerji did not introduce me to Jack Wayne and his publishing company; if Sarah Wayne were not the young woman with insight into life and its stories; if Susan Silva-Wayne did not have the sight for colors and shades of justice and injustice, my stories would have still remained untold. Thank you, Waynes.

A diligent and caring edit by Jennifer Day has preserved my stories and my voice.

This book has gone through many phases over a long time to become what it is now. Many great people have contributed to the growth of this book from memories to published stories.

Ghia Trusdale was an inspiring support and encouragement in the early days of this undertaking. Felice Bochman took the trouble to edit an earlier version of this manuscript, and put great effort into shaping and delivering marketable communications for publishing this book. I am grateful to them.

Masuda Sultan, the author of *My War at Home*, supported my efforts in publishing an earlier version of this book in my absence.

It was the partial personal fund I received from the Ministry of Citizenship and Immigration that gave me courage to initiate the project.

My family has never failed to be there for me, pouring their love and support in every phase of my life's journey.

My sister-in-law Dr. Malalai Sharif has been a supportive company and guard in this and all my professional endeavourers.

About the Author

Dr. Sharifa Sharif was born and raised in Afghanistan, where she and her family lived in many urban and rural areas.

Dr. Sharif studied Pashto literature in Kabul and, later, comparative literature in the United States, where she became immersed in learning about feminism, justice and freedom. Since then, she has become a dual Afghan-Canadian citizen and has worked as a writer, teacher, counselor for abused women, cultural advisor, radio host and politician.

Now living in the Greater Toronto Area, Dr. Sharif works as a community activist and cultural advisor on Afghanistan.